THE LIBRARIAN'S AND INFORMATION PROFESSIONAL'S

Guide to Plug-Ins and Other Web Browser Tools

SELECTION   INSTALLATION

TROUBLESHOOTING

Candice M. Benjes-Small and Melissa L. Just

Neal-Schuman Publishers, Inc.

New York   London

9523

Published by Neal-Schuman Publishers, Inc.
100 Varick Street
New York, NY 10013

The paper used in this publication meets the minimum requirements of American National Standard for Information Sciences—Permanence of Paper for Printed Library Materials, ANSI Z39, 48–1992.

ISBN 1-55570-441-7

Contents

List of Figures

Preface

Here's a quick quiz for today's busy professional.

Q: What are the following?
- Shockwave.
- iPix.
- QuickTime.
- MrSID.

A. Terms from the latest science fiction bestseller.
B. Evil devices used to consume bandwidth.
C. Ways to expand a Web browser's capabilities.
D. Internet things I wish I knew about but probably don't.

If you chose the last two options, *The Librarian's and Information Professional's Guide to Plug-Ins and Other Web Browser Tools: Selection, Installation, Troubleshooting* will help make sense of the hundreds of plug-ins, helper applications, ActiveX controls, and browser companions currently existing in the marketplace.

Librarians have become important players in this new virtual world by creating original Web sites, offering training and public access to the Internet, and making many professional uses of the World Wide Web. Clearly, it has become imperative for librarians to familiarize themselves with the innovative tools that can easily extend a Web browser's capabilities. This guide explores the most useful browser-extending tools currently available. It will help answer questions specifically pertinent to the library market. How do I decide which tools to install for patrons? Should I include plug-in-required features on a library site? Which tools would be most directly useful to librarians and other information professionals?

Before writing this book, we, the authors, were typical reference librarians eager to make full use of the Internet and struggling to help patrons effectively use Web sites. In those days, we were fascinated by the possibilities of plug-ins, but, frankly, we also considered them to be a constant source of headaches. Plug-ins caused many librarians to grumble, and we certainly did our fair share. There were so many plug-ins, and no one could figure out which ones to use, how to find and install them, or how to troubleshoot for problems that arise with them.

The idea for *The Librarian's and Information Professional's Guide to Plug-Ins and Other Web Browser Tools* began when a senior colleague pointed out that much of the everyday grumbling at our library could be traced to a lack of knowledge about plug-ins, and that a useful guide could be beneficial to librarians who do not have the time, technological know-how, or inclination to conduct the essential research on plug-ins. Knowing we could make a difference, we began diligently researching the topic.

It soon became apparent what a great help plug-ins could be for librarians! Library users are often enthusiastic about the interesting and entertaining items on the Web that are only available through plug-ins. Furthermore, there are plug-ins that might not be suitable for a public setting but are ideal for librarians on the job and in other professional endeavors. We quickly found that most plug-ins could be quite useful, tremendously enhancing Internet experiences. The fact that plug-ins aren't necessarily troublesome once they are understood was another wonderful discovery.

STRUCTURE

The plug-ins and other tools that we examine here are grouped into chapters by shared characteristics: image viewers, multimedia players, accessibility helpers, etc. Every chapter begins with an overview to the tools. Each tool's description contains the following elements:

Purpose
- This details why and how the plug-in can be of use for librarians or patrons. Past versions and a little bit of history of the tool is often included.

System Requirements
- This provides processor, operating system, and installed RAM re-

quirements, as well as information about browser compatibility and the program's file size. Not every tool has the same requirements, so there is some variation in these lists.

- Note: Internet Explorer 5.5 SP2 and 6 and Netscape Navigator 6.x Compatibility. Starting with service pack 2 for IE 5.5, Microsoft's browser no longer supports Netscape-style plug-ins. This left many plug-in developers scrambling to create IE-compatible ActiveX controls. Meanwhile Netscape Navigator 6 was released and had changed enough from previous versions of Netscape that many plug-ins that worked before could not be used in this latest release. This section clearly reports how well each plug-in has dealt with these changes.

Pros and Cons

- Every tool has its benefits and disadvantages; this is where both are described.

Examples

- Screenshots of Web pages using the plug-ins are found in each tool's description. Because plug-ins are often used to bring some vitality to static Web pages and are not at their best on the printed page, URLs are provided so that readers can visit the sites themselves.
- Note: A virtual tour of these tools is just a click away with the companion Web site available at www.book.candice.cc. Warning: the plug-in being exemplified will need to be installed for readers to fully appreciate the page!

Finding and Installing

- This will help explain how to locate the plug-in and put it onto a system. Finding is usually easy; installing can be more complicated. Luckily, more and more plug-ins are coming with installation wizards that walk the user through the process.

Troubleshooting

- Some of the most common problems that users experience with each plug-in are presented, as are suggested solutions.

Creating Files

- This section discusses how to create files for use with the plug-in. Sometimes the plug-in itself can be used to create files or perform file tasks.

Library Uses

- This section serves two purposes. First, it describes why a library might install the plug-in onto the institution's computers. Second, it suggests how libraries might take advantage of the technology to enliven their Web sites or provide interesting services to their patrons. Real library examples are provided.

ORGANIZATION

Chapter 1, "Essential Background of Browser-Extending Tools," provides an introduction to the types of tools discussed in the text including plug-ins, ActiveX controls, and helper applications, as well as the benefits and drawbacks of using these tools in libraries.

Chapter 2, "Utility Tools," begins the discussion of specific tools. Utilities that allow users to view text and other formatted files are introduced. The highlighted tools are Adobe Acrobat Reader, and Word, Excel, and PowerPoint viewers.

Chapter 3, "Image Tools," includes AlternaTIFF, iPIX, MrSID, Whip!, and VoloView.

Chapter 4, "Multimedia Tools," examines QuickTime, Shockwave, RealOne, Windows Media Player, and WinAMP—all useful tools that work with multimedia files. Additionally, a chart is provided to compare the viewers, their features, and best uses.

Chapter 5, "Math and Science Tools," introduces tools used to view and interact with scientific files. Chime, RasMol, and Cn3D are all tools used for three-dimensional molecular structures. LiveMath is used to view math files including algebra equations, graphs, and fractals.

Chapter 6, "Accessibility Tools," explores the tools important to consider when building Web-access computer stations as libraries strive to improve the accessibility of Web sites for disabled patrons. This chapter presents three tools of particular interest to libraries and librarians: Adobe Access, Lens Magnifying Glass, and ReadPlease.

Chapter 7, "Staff Tools for Librarians," focuses on tools that may be of particular interest to librarians for use on staff machines. Google Toolbar and Yahoo! Companion bring searching functionality to the Web browser toolbar, making it easier and faster to search the popular Web directory and search engine. Mousetool, a program designed to eliminate clicks of the mouse to help reduce repetitive stress injuries, and Pop-Up Stopper, a program that helps stop pop-up browser window advertisements from appearing, are also discussed in this chapter.

Chapter 8, "Strategies for Managing Plug-Ins," surveys key tools and best bets for the good management of them. Three programs, Plugsy,

Plug Master, and ActiveX Manager are all designed to help users manage the tools they have installed on their machines. Steps for successfully uninstalling tools are also discussed.

Three appendices complete *The Librarian's and Information Professional's Guide to Plug-Ins and Other Web Browser Tools.* They are:

Appendix A: "File Extensions," The guide to extensions and the programs that play them.

Appendix B: Troubleshooting Tips, The guide for common problems and all-purpose solutions.

Appendix C: Webliography, The guide for learning about and locating the right programs.

We hope the guide helps make sense of this fascinating but often confusing technical area. Good luck as you learn to make the best use of these tools. Soon you will be able to offer state-of-the-art Internet access to your library's staff and patrons with this step-by-step guide.

Acknowledgments

We would like to thank Janis F. Brown, Janet L. Nelson, Luis Franco, Jim Small, and all of the people who allowed their Web sites to serve as examples in this book.

Chapter 1

Essential Background of Browser-Extending Tools

OVERVIEW

Although users can accomplish more and more tasks on the Web, and access a growing number of file types, browsers themselves have not been the impetus for change. Netscape Navigator, Internet Explorer, and AOL browsers support only a small number of file formats: HTML documents and JPEG, GIF, and sometimes PNG graphics. Yet thanks to plug-ins and other browser add-ons, users can now watch videos, listen to music, and access Microsoft Office documents with their browsers.

Plug-ins and their cousins, ActiveX and helper applications, are programs that extend the power of the Web browser. When the browser runs across a file it cannot handle on its own, it will invoke the appropriate tool to open and read or play the file. Some of these tools are bundled with the browsers, but often the user must download the appropriate plug-in independently.

Users normally do not worry about plug-ins until they visit a Web page that requires a tool that is not on the machine. The most common sign that the user is missing a necessary component is an image of a puzzle piece where the file should be. Most sites will provide a link to download the necessary plug-in.

After installing the plugin, click here.

Figure 1-1. Sign of a Missing Plug-In
The puzzle piece indicates a necessary plug-in is not installed.

Library of Congress's American Memory Web site is a good example of a site that requires browser-extending tools. Although the majority of the information on it is simple text and graphics, which can be displayed in the browser, some collections contain files that need special viewers. Audio is available in Real, MP3, and WAV formats; some images are TIFF; maps require the MrSID Image Viewer; videos are in QuickTime's MOV, MPG, and Real's RM formats. Having these tools installed on the computer allows the user to see and hear a much more lively side of American history.

Library of Congress American Memory: Viewer Information
http://memory.loc.gov/ammem/film.html

American Memory Viewer Information

American Memory Film Collections	Quicktime Format	MPEG Format	Real Media Format
America at Work, America at Leisure: Motion Pictures from 1894-1915	*	*	*
The American Variety Stage: Vaudeville and Popular Entertainment, 1870-1920	*	*	*
Before and After the Great Earthquake and Fire: Early Films of San Francisco, 1897-1916	*	*	*
Buckaroos in Paradise: Ranching Culture in Northern Nevada, 1945-1982	*	*	*
Fifty Years of Coca-Cola Television Advertisements: Highlights from the Motion Picture Archives at the Library of Congress			*

Figure 1-2. Library of Congress's American Memory Collection
The American Memory site not only provides detailed information and links to different viewers, but also includes charts detailing what file format different collections use.

PLUG-INS VS. ACTIVEX VS. HELPER APPS VS. BROWSER COMPANIONS

Back when browsers were first around, people who wanted to view a file unsupported by the browser would need to open up another program. Just as someone who wanted to look at a Word document would need to open up Microsoft Word, a person who wanted to view a PDF would have to open up Acrobat Reader. But browsers became sophisticated enough to launch the file within the necessary program itself; clicking on a PDF link would automatically open the file in Reader. It would be in a separate window from the browser, but it would entail no work for the user. Browser-launched programs are known as helper applications.

In some instances this was not sufficient. A file might have a direct connection to the Web page that needed to be maintained—descriptive text describing a video, for example. Other times, the opening of a second window was confusing to Web users. When they were done reading the PDF file, they might not know to close the Reader and go back to the browser. For these types of situations, Web developers created plug-ins. Plug-ins are applications that are recognized by the browser and are fully integrated into the Web page.

Microsoft created its own type of plug-in with the development of ActiveX controls. ActiveX controls are small programs or animations for the Web; their chief advantage has been that these controls can be used in other Microsoft products. ActiveX controls work in Internet Explorer but not Netscape.

Then there are all the programs that don't quite fit into any of these categories but do enhance the browser experience. These could be called viewers or add-ons or browser-extending tools.

Of all these terms, "plug-in" is arguably the best known. In this book, the word "plug-in" will stand in for any tool that is downloaded and installed upon the user's computer and is meant to extend the browser's performance from the Web user's standpoint.

BENEFITS AND DISADVANTAGES OF BROWSER-EXTENDING TOOLS

Plug-ins have greatly increased the number of things a person can do on the Web. Many organizations would like to share existing files over either an intranet or on the Internet, but who would have the time to make those files Web-readable? Without plug-ins, the Web developer would have to convert all text documents into HTML before offering them online. The formatting of these papers would be primitive compared to their original layouts; HTML is limited in that capacity. Images would present other problems; high-resolution graphics would need to be turned into lower-end GIFs and JPGs. And whenever a change to text or images was made, the organization would need to make sure both the print and the Web versions reflect that change. Many library sites do operate on this system, and any of the people responsible for those sites can tell you how challenging it is.

But with Adobe Acrobat, existing files can be easily turned into PDF files. Print documents can be scanned into a computer and then made into PDFs. Microsoft Office documents can be hyperlinked into Web pages now. The only catch? Users can only access the PDF and the Office documents if they have the correct plug-in on their computer.

As the Web has grown, serious attention has been paid as to how best to attract and keep an audience. Multimedia has offered a more interesting Web, one in which users can watch movie trailers before the trailers appear in theatres; one in which students can participate in online tutorials; one in which potential buyers can listen to a music CD before purchasing it. People are raising their expectations of what Web sites should offer, and that usually leads to features requiring plug-ins.

So if developers are creating files that need plug-ins, and users enjoy these files, what is the problem? The downside of plug-ins resides in the maintenance of these tools. For librarians in charge of public access stations, this is a major concern.

The only thing reliable about plug-ins is that they will change. As soon as a plug-in is released, the developers are usually working on the next version. New iterations may come out once a month or once a year. The former is more likely. This is why plug-ins often have version numbers with a couple of decimal points—numerous variations of a version are released before it is "new" enough to deserve an upgrade to the next whole number. A visit to many plug-in sites will offer the user a chance to download the latest version, a beta version (something that is being tested as an improvement over the official version), and maybe an alpha version (the developers are pretty sure the beta version works but are not quite ready to release it as the official new version).

When a new version is released, the plug-in developers would like everyone to upgrade to it. The most effective way is to make sure that products created for the plug-in will only work if the user has the most current version. A user could visit a site that requires Shockwave, and if he does not have the most up-to-date version, it will not work. Luckily, more and more plug-ins now have a built-in feature that has them automatically check to see if there is an upgrade available. The user in such a situation would have to wait a few minutes while Shockwave upgrades itself, but this is immensely easier than uninstalling the old version, finding the Shockwave site, and then locating how to download and install the new player.

If a plug-in is not updated within a year, there is a good chance it never will be. Many plug-ins are created by volunteers (especially engineering and computer science students) who release their program and then move on to other projects. Sometimes the plug-in is created by a company that disappears in one of the dot-com crashes. Or a plug-in is bought by a competitor, and then vanishes. Customer support, if ever present, disappears, and no new versions are released. It is pure luck if the plug-in continues to work with later operating systems and browsers. This book tried to choose plug-ins that have stable backgrounds and promise to be around for a while, but in the world of the Web, there are no guarantees.

Some plug-ins, particularly the multimedia players, have a bad reputation as bandwidth hogs. Video files can be extremely large. However, developers usually try to make their files small enough for downloading over a modem. Further, the emergence of Napster and its like have shown what real bandwidth hogs look like, and people don't tend to look at the multimedia players as unfavorably.

Plug-ins do not always cooperate with one another. The multimedia chapter details how these players can confuse a computer with their fights for dominance. Other plug-ins may fight over sharing file space. Still others are unstable and may crash a computer continuously. There are few guarantees in the plug-in world; users who install these programs onto their machines are gambling that it will work—and that if it doesn't, the user can figure out how to fix it.

There are librarians who take the stance that plug-ins are more hassle than they are worth and refuse to put them on public machines. They invest in computer software security, erase any plug-ins that somehow sneak onto computers, and tell users who want to view unusual files that they will have to go elsewhere.

The other school of thought is that plug-ins are a worthwhile challenge. Librarians whose priority is to help patrons find information need to know that plug-ins can provide access to items in an unusual format. Many people think the files that need plug-ins are frivolous entertainment, but as this book's authors found, there is a treasure trove of knowledge locked behind the plug-in gates: CNN videos of historic events; rare audio files of the long dead; pictorial maps that cannot be displayed in standard browsers; interactive tutorials for software programs; 3D views of chemical compounds, which can be turned and revolved by users. It is a magical world beyond the static Web of HTML.

Chapter 2

Utility Tools

OVERVIEW

Displaying highly formatted documents with complex layout on the Web can be a difficult and time-consuming task. Documents with text in columns, multiple fonts, complex graphics with captions or wrapped wording, stylized tables, and other carefully constructed layout elements cannot be faithfully reproduced in HTML. Even with advanced HTML skills and nonstandard work-arounds such as using an invisible pixel image to create paragraphing tabs, and knowledge of Cascading Style Sheets, the exact look of a document cannot be guaranteed. At times, it is necessary and desirable to distribute documents in their native format.

This chapter addresses four types of complex documents: Microsoft Word, Excel, PowerPoint, and Portable Document Format (PDF).

The Microsoft Office suite of software, including Word, Excel, and PowerPoint is standard in most work environments. Libraries produce many documents using these tools including library guides, handouts, class presentations, newsletters, library card applications, budgets, and more. Many of these documents are appropriate to distribute on the library's Web site in addition to being made available in print in the library. However, Microsoft Office does not come standard on most home computer systems. Users must purchase the software suite at a substantial cost. Libraries that decide to distribute Word, Excel, or PowerPoint files on the Web need to be aware of the potential limitations of users' machines.

One way to overcome users' lack of software is to distribute, or link to, read-only versions of Office programs that are freely available. With these Microsoft Office viewers installed on their computers, users are able to view documents even if they do not own the correct Office program. Libraries providing Office documents on their Web sites should be sure to provide a link to the appropriate site for downloading these viewers.

Another option for libraries is to convert all Office documents into PDF files using the full version of Adobe Acrobat. With Acrobat, any Office document can be made into a PDF file with a simple save or export command. Providing all Office documents as PDF has two benefits. First, users will only have to install one plug-in. Adobe Acrobat will display them all. This is especially important to Macintosh users since there is not a Macintosh version of the Word or Excel Viewer. The second benefit is that documents that are distributed as PDF are more difficult to copy. Although the newest version of Adobe Acrobat reader does allow users to copy and paste text from PDF files into other programs, the document owner can turn off the feature during conversion.

In addition to being an easy way for libraries to distribute documents, PDF files are a standard format for viewing online journals from full-text databases and publisher's Web sites. Since many other Web documents are also available in PDF many users will already have the Reader installed on their home machines. For public and staff stations within libraries, Adobe Acrobat is an essential tool.

This chapter will illustrate the usefulness of document utilities and highlight their role in the library Web environment.

ADOBE ACROBAT READER

Purpose

Adobe Acrobat is a document viewer that allows users to view Portable Document Format (PDF) files. PDF files are created to allow users to easily share documents, regardless of computer platform or installed software. For example, a Microsoft Word document created on a Windows machine running Word 2000 may not be readable by a Macintosh user running an older version of Word. That same file converted to PDF would be universally readable. In addition, PDF conversion retains the original document formatting including layout, fonts, graphics, and color.

The plug-in portion of the software is the Adobe Acrobat Reader. Version 5 of Acrobat Reader is freely available for Windows and Macintosh platforms. Palm OS support has also been added in this release. The main functions of the plug-in are to view, print, and save PDF files. Other optional features, including the ability to view thumbnails of pages and fill out forms online for printing, may sometimes be available. The PDF file creator determines the availability of these options.

If programmed correctly, PDF files created in version 5 have the ability to resize to fit the screen. This is useful when viewing PDF files on the Personal Digital Assistants (PDAs), which have much smaller screens than desktop or laptop computers. Another new feature is the ability to create PDF with imbedded mark-up that allows for better document flow for screen reading software. These marked-up PDF files will help libraries comply with ADA accessibility issues.

System Requirements

Processor:	Pentium PC; PowerPC Macintosh
Operating Systems:	Microsoft Windows 95 OSR 2.0, Windows 98, Windows Millennium, Windows NT 4.0 with Service Pack 5 or 6, or Windows 2000; Mac OS software version 8.6, 9.0.4, or 9.1
Installed RAM:	32 MB of RAM (64 MB recommended)
Browsers:	Netscape 4.X or greater, Microsoft Internet Explorer 4.X or greater
Hard Disk Space:	24 MB of available hard-disk space (70 additional MB required for optional Chinese, Japanese, and Korean fonts)

Internet Explorer 5.5 SP2 and 6.0 and Netscape 6.X Compatibility

Adobe Acrobat Reader is compatible with later versions of Internet Explorer. Adobe began including an ActiveX control in Reader version 4.0 to allow Acrobat files to open within the Internet Explorer window. There are no known conflicts with Netscape 6.X.

Pros and Cons

The biggest benefit of Adobe Acrobat Reader is that it provides a way for libraries to deliver documents to most users, regardless of platform. Fliers, handouts, announcements, etc. can be placed on the Web without jeopardizing the layout of the documents. Although the content could be converted to HTML, the subsequent pages probably would not print as nicely or compactly.

Because most users will have only the Acrobat Reader installed, the PDF files will be read-only, preventing users from editing the delivered content. Although some users may believe this is a "con," most librarians will find comfort in this small amount of file control. Documents converted to PDF files are also unlikely to contain viruses. Although it is possible for a PDF file to contain a virus, only files transmitted via the Microsoft Outlook e-mail system and opened using the full version of Adobe Acrobat will spread the virus.

One drawback of the Acrobat Reader is that users who use the fill-out form feature often want to save their filled-out form. Upon saving, the PDF file loses its user customization. The form fill-out feature is useful only when printing.

Examples

Internal Revenue Service Forms and Publications

www.irs.gov/forms_pubs/fillin.html

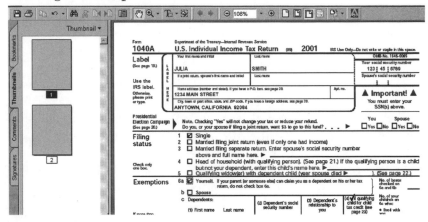

Figure 2-1. Internal Revenue Service Forms in PDF
The IRS provides online forms for taxes, many of which have the fill-in feature enabled. The Text tool icon on the Adobe Acrobat screen turns the feature on and off and placing the cursor in the form and typing fills it in. Check boxes are selected by clicking on the desired boxes. Thumbnails also provide a preview of the number of pages.

Statistical Abstract of the United States

www.census.gov/prod/2002pubs/01statab/stat-ab01.html

No. 239. Public School Employment: 1982 and 1998

[In thousands (3,082 represents 3,082,000). Covers full-time employment. Excludes Hawaii. 1982 also excludes District of Columbia and New Jersey. 1982 based on sample survey of school districts with 250 or more students. 1998 based on sample survey of school districts with 100 or more employees; see source for sampling variability]

Occupation	1982					1998				
	Total	Male	Female	White [1]	Black [1]	Total	Male	Female	White [1]	Black [1]
All occupations	3,082	1,063	2,019	2,498	432	3,890	1,040	2,850	3,028	515
Officials, administrators	41	31	10	36	3	50	27	23	42	5
Principals and assistant principals	90	72	19	78	11	105	53	52	81	16
Classroom teachers [2]	1,680	534	1,146	1,435	186	2,157	544	1,613	1,805	208
Elementary schools	798	129	669	667	98	1,079	151	928	895	103
Secondary schools	706	363	343	619	67	795	331	464	677	73
Other professional staff	235	91	144	193	35	277	61	216	228	32
Teachers aides [3]	215	14	200	146	45	389	43	346	257	78
Clerical, secretarial staff	210	4	206	177	19	266	11	255	203	29
Service workers [4]	611	316	295	434	132	646	301	345	411	147

[1] Excludes individuals of Hispanic origin. [2] Includes other classroom teachers, not shown separately. [3] Includes technicians. [4] Includes craftworkers and laborers.

Source: U.S. Equal Employment Opportunity Commission, *Elementary-Secondary Staff Information (EEO-5)*, biennial.

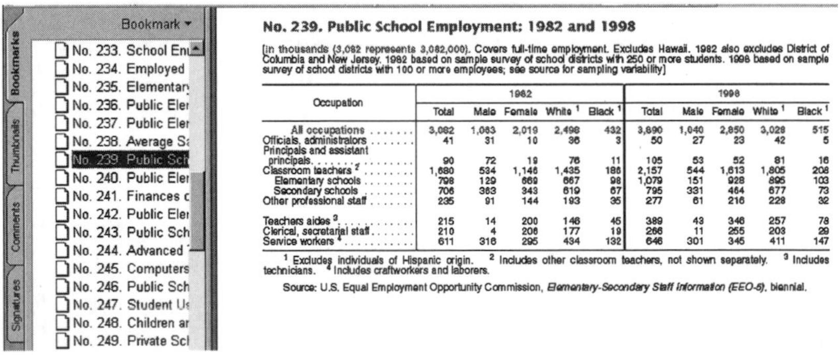

Figure 2-2. Bookmarks in the 2001 Statistical Abstract of the United States
Bookmarks serve as table of contents links to jump to a desired section of a PDF document.

INTERNET PUBLIC LIBRARY WEB SITE

www.ipl.org

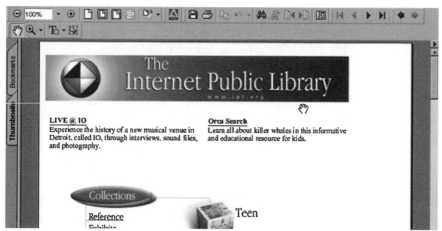

Figure 2-3. The Internet Public Library Home Page
Courtesy of the Internet Public Library
The Internet Public Library home page was converted to PDF using Adobe's "Create Adobe PDF Online" feature. The converted document retains its hyperlinks and formatting.

Finding and Installing

Because it is the de facto standard for document delivery on the Web, the Acrobat Reader often comes installed on new computer systems.

The Acrobat Reader is free and can be downloaded from Adobe's Web site at www.adobe.com. The Adobe Acrobat program can be purchased if PDF file creation is desired. Adobe charges $249.00 when purchasing on their Web Site.

Troubleshooting

Problem: On some stations, PDF files load within the browser window. On others, the PDF files load in the Acrobat Reader software in a separate window. How can I choose which setup I want?

Solution: Open the Acrobat Reader software. From the Edit menu, select Preferences, then Options. Check or uncheck the Display PDF in Browser option depending on which display format you prefer.

Problem: The PDF file I downloaded from the Web won't display properly in Acrobat Reader.

Solution: Are you using the most recent version of Acrobat Reader? Files created in newer versions of the software sometimes do not display properly unless you have the most recent version.

Problem: My browser displays a blank window when I try to view a PDF file. I'm using Internet Explorer v5.0 on a PC.

Solution: Installing IE version 5.01 service pack will solve this problem. Another solution is to save each Acrobat file instead of trying to open it in Acrobat from the Web. To do this, right-click on the link to the file and choose "Save Target As..." to save the file on your computer, then open it in Acrobat.

Creating Files

Although the Acrobat Reader is free, the complete Adobe Acrobat commercial software program is required to create PDF files.

PDF files can be created from within any other program. The Adobe Acrobat software works as a print manager that converts PostScript files into PDF. In Microsoft Office programs, a Print PDF menu option makes PDF creation quick and easy. Other programs simply require users to print to the Adobe PDF Writer or Distiller on the print screen to convert documents to PDF.

Another option for PDF creation is the "Create Adobe PDF Online" feature on Adobe's Web site. This feature allows subscribers to submit Microsoft Office, WordPerfect, Image, Adobe program, or PostScript files, or HTML pages, which will be converted and delivered via Web browser or e-mail. Online conversion subscriptions cost $9.99/month or $99.99/year and include unlimited document conversion. Create Adobe PDF Online is available at www.adobe.com/store/products/ createpdf.html.

Library Uses

The typical use in a library setting is the Web distribution of printed materials: flyers, schedules, reading guides, printable library card applications, and documents in non-Roman foreign languages that do not easily display on the Web. Much of this material often duplicates information on the site in HTML format, but PDF versions are preferred for reading offline. Printed PDF files are usually shorter and more attractive than printed HTML formats. For printing forms to fill out, PDF is the only format that will assure proper alignment on the printed page.

Academic libraries may use the PDF format extensively for remote distribution of e-reserve items. Instead of being in the library, checking out the reserve materials, and copying or reading the items in the one- or two-hour checkout period, scanned articles or books' chapters placed on the Web can be printed quickly and usually less expensively than photocopying. Also, the online format allows more than one user to access high demand items (no waiting two hours for another patron to return checked-out items).

MICROSOFT OFFICE VIEWERS

Purpose

Microsoft Office Viewers for Word, Excel, and PowerPoint are pared-down versions of their commercial counterparts that allow users to view and print Microsoft Office files without owning the Office programs. Although most computers in the workplace, in academic computing labs, and in library computing facilities provide access to this suite of software, many home users do not own these three ubiquitous yet costly software tools. The Microsoft Office Viewers are built for them.

The viewers are freely downloadable from the Web and are easy to install. They allow users to share documents with other users who do not own Word, Excel, or PowerPoint. The viewers do not allow for the editing or saving of documents, however—users can copy from the Office document and paste into other applications.

The three viewers were all built for the Office 97 versions of documents but also have been updated to support Office 2000.

System Requirements

Processor:	Windows PC with at least a 486 processor; PowerPC processor-based Macintosh
Operating Systems:	Windows 95 or later; Apple System 7.5 or later
Installed RAM:	Word: At least 8 MB; 12 MB required for Windows NT stations
	Excel: At least 8 MB; 16 MB required for Windows NT stations
	PowerPoint: At least 16 MB
Browsers:	Netscape 3.X or greater, Microsoft Internet Explorer 3.X or greater, AOL 3.0 or greater
File Size:	Word Viewer: 38.6MB
	Excel Viewer: 38.13MB
	PowerPoint Viewer for Windows: 28.26MB
	PowerPoint Viewer for Macintosh: 6.5MB

Internet Explorer 5.5 SP2 and 6.0 and Netscape 6.X Compatibility

Since they are all Microsoft products with support for ActiveX, the Word, Excel, and PowerPoint viewers are all compatible with later versions of Internet Explorer. There are no known conflicts with Netscape 6.X.

Pros and Cons

The biggest benefit of the Microsoft Office Viewers is the ability for users to share documents with colleagues and libraries to share documents with patrons. Although saving is not an option, the content of the documents can be captured with the copy and paste features in the viewers.

Because the programs do not allow macros, the ability to spread viruses when sharing documents is decreased. This is particularly beneficial in libraries with Internet stations that allow access to e-mail and e-mail attachments. Patrons who open infected Microsoft attachments are less likely to infect the workstation.

Another benefit of the viewer suite is the fact that Microsoft encourages the distribution of the software. Libraries can provide local downloads of the tools from their own Web page and Web server instead of sending patrons off to another Web site. With local downloads, the library's Web manager will not have to worry about the URL of the download site changing or disappearing.

The biggest drawback at the moment is the lack of Macintosh versions of the Word and Excel Viewers. Macintosh users are unable to download and view files unless they own the full version of the software.

Examples

FEDERAL EMERGENCY MANAGEMENT AGENCY

www.fema.gov/emi/cert/examp.htm

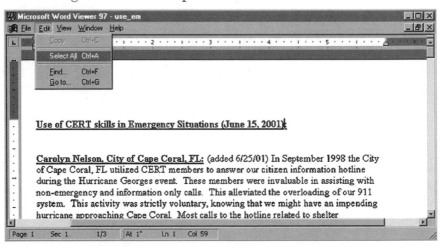

Figure 2-4. Federal Emergency Management Agency's Documents in Word
FEMA provides many of its documents in Word format, including this file that describes the use of Community Emergency Response Teams in emergency situations. When using Netscape Navigator, the viewers launch as separate helper applications.

US Government Printing Office

w3.access.gpo.gov/usbudget/fy2001/summary.html

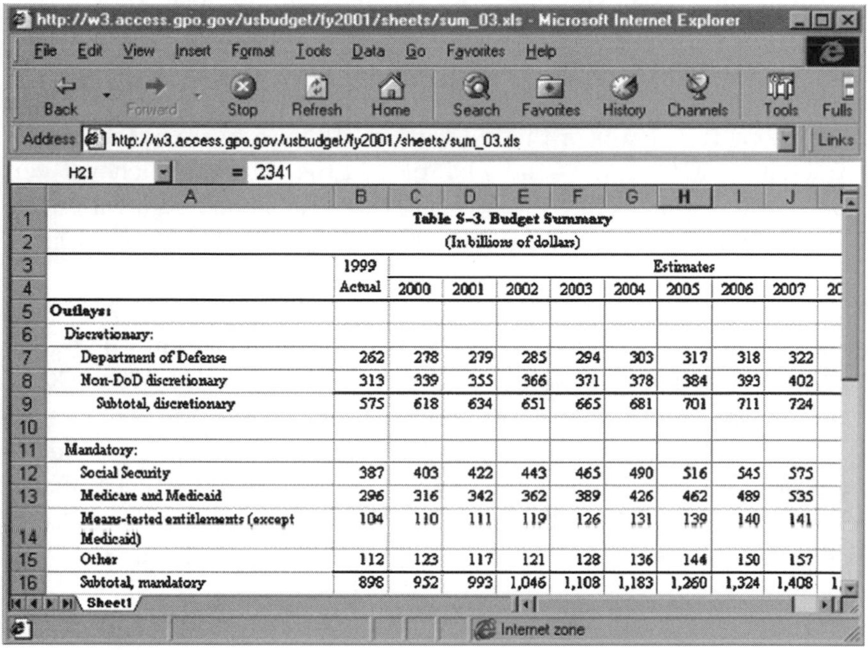

	1999 Actual	2000	2001	2002	2003	2004	2005	2006	2007	20
Table S–3. Budget Summary (In billions of dollars)		Estimates								
Outlays:										
Discretionary:										
Department of Defense	262	278	279	285	294	303	317	318	322	
Non-DoD discretionary	313	339	355	366	371	378	384	393	402	
Subtotal, discretionary	575	618	634	651	665	681	701	711	724	
Mandatory:										
Social Security	387	403	422	443	465	490	516	545	575	
Medicare and Medicaid	296	316	342	362	389	426	462	489	535	
Means-tested entitlements (except Medicaid)	104	110	111	119	126	131	139	140	141	
Other	112	123	117	121	128	136	144	150	157	
Subtotal, mandatory	898	952	993	1,046	1,108	1,183	1,260	1,324	1,408	1,

Figure 2-5. United States's Budget in Excel
The budget of the United States is made available through the Government Printing Office Web site. Each budgetary element is provided in either Microsoft Excel or Lotus 1-2-3 formats. When using Internet Explorer, the viewer opens the document within the browser window.

Finding and Installing

The viewers are all available for download from the Microsoft site. Follow the steps below for the appropriate viewer.

Windows—office.microsoft.com/downloads/default.aspx

Under Product pull-down menu, select Word, Excel, or PowerPoint. Select All Versions under the Version pull-down menu. Check the yellow box to retrieve Converters and Viewers. The files to download are Word 97/2000 Viewer (Word 2000) (Windows 95/98/NT), Excel 97/2000 Viewer: Spreadsheet Files, and PowerPoint Viewer 97 (2000 Release) for PowerPoint 2000 Users.

MACINTOSH—WWW.MICROSOFT.COM/MAC/DOWNLOAD/OFFICE98/ POWERPOINT98VIEWER.ASP

Only the PowerPoint viewer is available in Macintosh format.

When installing the viewers on machines that already have the full version of the software installed (testing purposes, installing viewers for a more current version), the installation process may include the option of selecting the viewer or the full version of the software as the default launcher for DOC, XLS, and PPT files in the future. Whichever version selected will become the program that is launched both within the browser and whenever users double-click to open a file located locally.

Troubleshooting

Problem: I had the Word (or Excel) Viewer installed and just upgraded to the full version of the software. All of my files with a DOC (XLS) extension still launch the viewer only.

Solution: Your registry still recognizes Word (Excel) Viewer as the default program for running DOC (XLS) files. Uninstall the Word (Excel) Viewer then open the full version of Word (Excel). This should reset your registry to recognize Word (Excel) as the default program for DOC (XLS) files.

Problem: I'm trying to view a Microsoft Excel 97 file on my Macintosh. Where can I get a viewer?

Solution: Unfortunately, the Microsoft viewers for Word and Excel are not available in a Macintosh format. However, Windows users can use the Windows version of the viewers to see Word and Excel files created with the Mac version of the software.

Problem: I need to print a PowerPoint presentation in "handout" format. How do I change the print settings?

Solution: The PowerPoint Viewer provides limited features including viewing a presentation and printing. However, the printing feature only allows you to print in the "slide" format, with one slide per page.

Creating Files

Microsoft files to be distributed over the Internet should be created in the usual fashion using the full version of the appropriate Microsoft Office product.

Library Uses

A common use for Microsoft Office Viewers in academic libraries is for electronic reserves. Instructors can make information available to students via an electronic reserves system such as Docutek's ERes system.

Instructors can place items such as course handouts, notes, presentations, and spreadsheets on the Web for enrolled students to access. Microsoft Viewers allow the students to read the information in its native format without having to purchase costly software and also allow the instructors to place materials on the Web without having to convert files to other formats such as PDF. The ERes system provides links that libraries can customize that will point students to a place to download the necessary plug-ins, including the Microsoft Office Viewers.

WORD

Community libraries often become repositories of information about their towns and surrounding areas and provide archival or historical information to their patrons. These documents are usually gathered from resources outside of the library and exist in many formats. Libraries who wish to provide access to these materials electronically may provide them in their native format or convert the documents. The Hubbard Public Library in Hubbard, Ohio, provides links to historical documents about its town at www.hubbard.lib.oh.us/HPL_Pages/action/Files.htm, including transcripts from an oral history project, a brief history of the town, information about Hubbard families, and town activities such as Pioneer Days. Some of these documents have been converted to PDF format, but many are only available as Word documents. The Hubbard library site includes a link to download the free Microsoft Word Viewer.

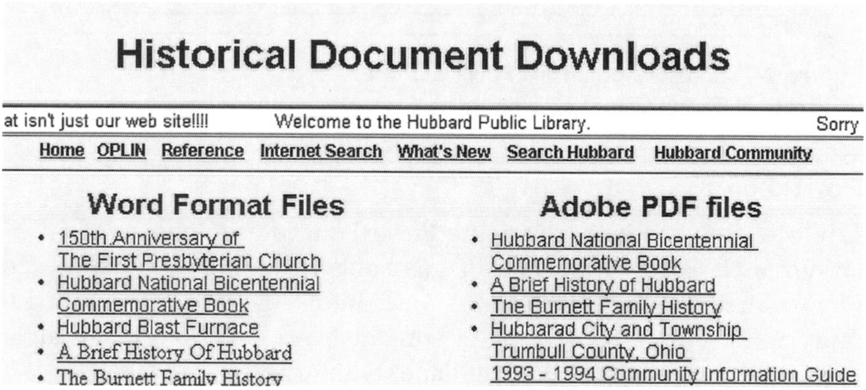

Historical Document Downloads

at isn't just our web site!!!!   Welcome to the Hubbard Public Library.   Sorry

Home   OPLIN   Reference   Internet Search   What's New   Search Hubbard   Hubbard Community

Word Format Files

- 150th Anniversary of The First Presbyterian Church
- Hubbard National Bicentennial Commemorative Book
- Hubbard Blast Furnace
- A Brief History Of Hubbard
- The Burnett Family History

Adobe PDF files

- Hubbard National Bicentennial Commemorative Book
- A Brief History of Hubbard
- The Burnett Family History
- Hubbarad City and Township Trumbull County, Ohio 1993 - 1994 Community Information Guide

Figure 2-6. Word Documents at the Hubbard Public Library
This site is created by the Hubbard Public Library and cannot be reprinted without permission.

EXCEL

Microsoft Excel is often used to produce financial reports and statistics. Many libraries, especially libraries that are publicly funded are required to provide this information. The Indiana State Library is an example of a library that provides annual statistics to the public at www.statelib.lib.in.us/WWW/LDO/Statsmenu00.htm.

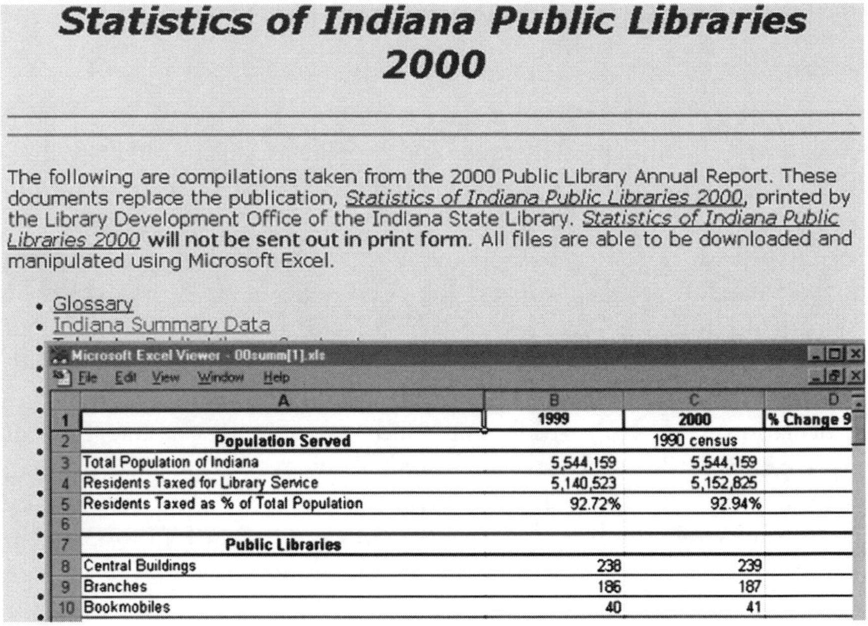

Statistics of Indiana Public Libraries 2000

The following are compilations taken from the 2000 Public Library Annual Report. These documents replace the publication, *Statistics of Indiana Public Libraries 2000*, printed by the Library Development Office of the Indiana State Library. *Statistics of Indiana Public Libraries 2000* **will not be sent out in print form.** All files are able to be downloaded and manipulated using Microsoft Excel.

- Glossary
- Indiana Summary Data

Microsoft Excel Viewer - 00summ[1].xls

File   Edit   View   Window   Help

A	B	C	D
1	1999	2000	% Change 9
2 Population Served		1990 census	
3 Total Population of Indiana	5,544,159	5,544,159	
4 Residents Taxed for Library Service	5,140,523	5,152,825	
5 Residents Taxed as % of Total Population	92.72%	92.94%	
6			
7 Public Libraries			
8 Central Buildings	238	239	
9 Branches	186	187	
10 Bookmobiles	40	41	

Figure 2-7. Statistics of Indiana Public Libraries
Courtesy of the Indiana State Library

POWERPOINT

Libraries may choose to distribute PowerPoint presentations for orientations or classes to students who are unable to attend or are interested in more time-of-need information. For example, the Danbury Public Library in Danbury, Connecticut, has placed its presentation "Get Caught in the Web!" on their Web site at danburylibrary.org/powerpoint.

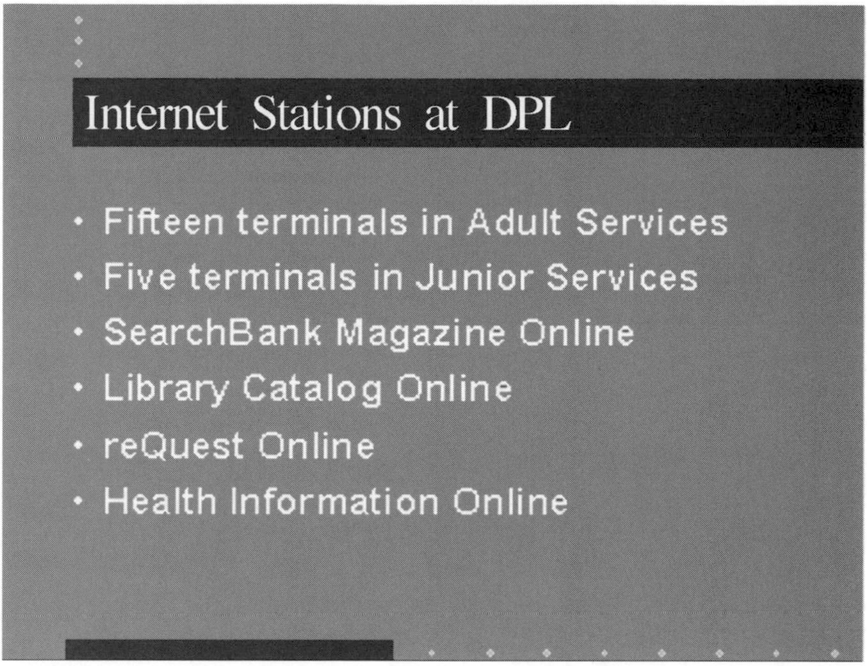

Figure 2-8. PowerPoint Slide from the Danbury Public Library
Courtesy of the Danbury Public Library

Chapter 3

Image Tools

OVERVIEW

Graphics are an integral and powerful part of the Web browsing experience. They add style, balance, and impact to Web pages and even help with navigation. Typical Web graphics come from one of three sources: 1) they are converted from paper sources including photographs or other documents; 2) they are digital photos captured with a digital camera or other recording device; or 3) they are images that have been created from a graphics software program such as PhotoShop. Most graphics on the Web are static, but some are animated, usually with animated GIF technology, the digital equivalent of a paper flipbook. All are GIF or JPEG images and are one-dimensional.

With plug-ins, more advanced image technology is possible. Some image formats allow users to pan to move left and right and up and down, or to zoom in and out to get a better view of a particular part of an image. Other image formats include layers (like transparencies) that can be turned on and off to view how pieces lay on top of one another to build the whole image. Many legacy-system image databases produce images in formats other than GIF or JPEG that cannot be viewed within the standard Web browser setup. Web site developers who wish to incorporate more advanced imagery in their Web pages must rely on other graphics technology and use different tools.

This chapter examines four tools used to view, create, print, and interact with graphics. Each of the tools highlighted has a unique role. None of these tools open and display the same file formats. However, each has a place in the library computing environment, either on users' desktops in the library or as tools for patrons to use to view content delivered by the library.

ALTERNATIFF

Purpose

AlternaTIFF, a Netscape-style plug-in developed by Medical Informatics Engineering (MIE), allows Web users to view TIFF files through their browsers. TIFF is a graphics file format that allows a high-level of resolution with little or no compression of the size of the image. Many programs, including Microsoft Word and PowerPoint, can read the TIFF format. It is relatively easy to scan a paper document and save it as a TIFF, and numerous institutions have taken this step to place their documents online. For some consortiums, such as patent offices, TIFF is the international standard and all files must be in this format. Some Web sites that allow users to receive faxes over the Web provide the documents as TIFFs. These TIFF files cannot be viewed in current Web browsers, which are limited to GIF, JPG, and sometimes PNG graphic file formats. Unfortunately, sometimes the document provider cannot afford the financial or personnel resources to convert these TIFF files into a Web-readable format. Instead, the Web user must find an appropriate plug-in that will allow viewing of the file, such as AlternaTIFF.

System Requirements

Processor:	Pentium 150
Operating Systems:	Windows 95 or higher
Installed RAM:	.5MB
Browsers:	Netscape 3X and higher; Internet Explorer 3X and higher
File Size:	210KB

Internet Explorer 5.5 SP2 and 6.0 and Netscape Navigator 6.X Compatibility

AlternaTIFF is a good example of the Netscape-style plug-in that the most recent versions of Internet Explorer no longer support. MIE created an ActiveX AlternaTIFF to alleviate the situation. The homepage for AlternaTIFF, www.alternatiff.com, has a detailed chart indicating which plug-in version should be installed depending on the user's browser. There are no known conflicts with Netscape 6.X.

Pros and Cons

AlternaTIFF has garnered praise for being free, relatively small, and very easy to install. Its Web site is full of information about the plug-in, plans for improvements, and troubleshooting tips.

Other programs, such as Apple's QuickTime, can read TIFF files, but few do it as simply as AlternaTIFF. Some users have reported QuickTime can have trouble opening up large TIFFs that AlternaTIFF handles with ease. As AlternaTIFF is PC-only, Macintosh users will need to use QuickTime.

The biggest drawback to using AlternaTIFF is its difficulties with Internet Explorer. Even earlier versions of the browser have had trouble working with the plug-in. In some cases, users may be directed to save the TIFF to the desktop and open it with an offline program such as Imaging for Windows. Computers with Windows 95 or later will have this program under the Start/Accessories menu.

Examples

NATIONAL WEATHER SERVICE

weather.noaa.gov/pub/fax/PGBE99.TIF

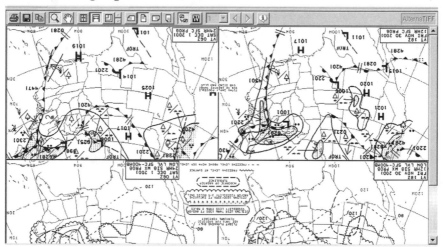

Figure 3-1. National Weather Service Charts in TIFF Format
Facsimile weather charts are available from the National Weather Service in TIFF format. The original file is upside down; the AlternaTIFF toolbar has an icon to flip images 90- and 180-degrees.

UNITED STATES PATENT OFFICE

www.uspto.gov

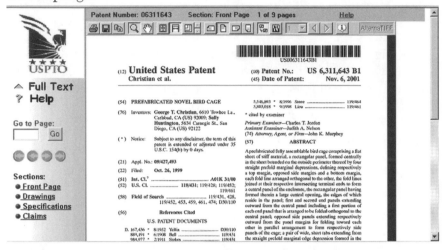

Figure 3-2. United States Patent Office Web Site
Users may view TIFF images of US patents online through the United States Patent Office Web site. This site launches AlternaTIFF within the browser rather than outside, as happened in the first example.

VIRGINIA DIGITAL LIBRARY

eagle.vsla.edu/conpen

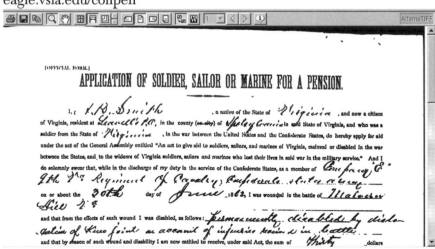

Figure 3-3. Confederate Pension Applications for Veterans and Widows
Courtesy of the Library of Virginia's Digital Library Program
The Confederate Pension Applications for Veterans and Widows is located in the Virginia Digital Library site. Users can search by surname and view TIFF images of the applications from 1888, 1900, and 1912.

Finding and Installing

Go to the AlternaTIFF site at www.alternatiff.com to install or upgrade this plug-in. A detailed chart helps the user decide which version of the plug-in will work best with his environment. Dialog boxes will walk users through the installation process, and AlternaTIFF suggests most users will wish to retain the default settings. Registration is required for single users.

If many computer stations need AlternaTIFF, consider a site license. At $10 per copy (minimum of 20 copies) it may be beyond the library's budget, but it does not require registration and all upgrades and e-mail support are free.

Troubleshooting

Problem: I'm using Internet Explorer and only get a black or gray rectangle in the AlternaTIFF window.

Solution: As previously mentioned, AlternaTIFF and IE have difficulty working together. The easiest solution is to use Netscape 4.X. If that is not viable, try upgrading to AlternaTIFF beta version 1.40b3. For more advanced techniques, see the FAQ on the AlternaTIFF site at www.alternatiff.com/faq.html.

Problem: I would like to use AlternaTIFF to view TIFF files, but Apple's QuickTime automatically opens when I try to access a TIFF.

Solution: If you let it, QuickTime would try to read just about every file type you view—no matter how well it can actually accomplish the task. QuickTime 4 and later releases allow you access to the control panel; from there, you can turn off support for TIFF files.

Problem: I would like to use AlternaTIFF to view TIFF files, but another plug-in (not QuickTime 4 or later) automatically opens when I try to access a TIFF.

Solution: First, see if you can turn off support for TIFF in the other plug-in. File support options are usually located in Preferences. If you have no use for the plug-in, you can remove or rename it. In the Netscape directory structure, you can find the plug-ins in: Program Files\Netscape\Communicator\Plugins.

If you wish to continue using these plug-ins, you can try a plug-in manager like Plugsy.

Problem: How do I control the amount AlternaTIFF zooms in on an image?

Solution: Currently, the only way to change the size of the TIFF beyond full-size or zoom is to change the monitor settings.

Creating Files

TIFF files can be created with any graphics program, from the high-end Adobe Photoshop, www.adobe.com, to the freely distributed GIMP, www.gimp.org, and everything in between. These same programs can be used to convert TIFF files into GIF or JPG.

Library Uses

If at all possible, libraries should not put TIFF files onto their public site. The TIFF format adds little if anything to the Web experience; users would be better served with a GIF or JPG image. As the AlternaTIFF Web site's disclaimer says, "This program is not intended to encourage the use of the TIFF file format as a standard for image exchange. We wrote AlternaTIFF out of necessity, not because we like TIFF." If retaining image quality is of the highest importance, consider using Adobe Acrobat to create a PDF file. The image may be fuzzy on the screen, but the page will print beautifully.

Cornell University Library has numerous TIFF documents in its digital library that it wished to share on the Web. Rather than require a plug-in for viewing, the TIFF files are converted on the fly into GIFs using a software package called tif2gif. Libraries interested in providing access to TIFF images can read more about the tif2gif package at its Web site, kalex.engin.umich.edu/tif2gif.

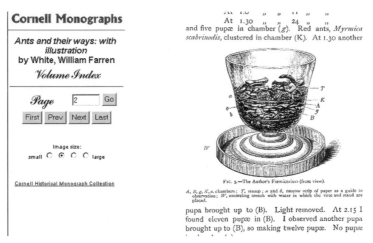

Figure 3-4. Cornell Monographs's TIFF Version of the Book *Ants and Their Ways* Courtesy of the Cornell University Library Making of America Digital Collection Cornell Digital Library, cdl.library.cornell.edu, has scanned damaged books into TIFF format as a form of preservation. The left-hand frame provides navigation; the scanned book pages appear in the right-hand frame.

Some libraries will send and receive interlibrary loan articles electronically in TIFF format. When sending these documents on to users, it is important to tell the recipients about AlternaTIFF and Imaging for Windows.

IPIX VIEWER

Purpose

Internet Pictures (iPIX) provides a 3D experience on the Web. When looking at an iPIX image, users can click their mouse to look up, down, left, right, and turn around in a full circle, 360 degrees by 360 degrees. It is as if the user is in the middle of the view being shown. iPIX calls this "immersive imaging." Done well, the iPIX image gives the illusion of being a part of the picture.

iPIX viewers were originally created for offline use; the viewer would be sent to a helper application outside of the Web browser in order to see the file. The current version is entitled "iPIX Plug-In and Viewer" and opens the iPIX file directly in Netscape or Internet Explorer. In August 2001, the company announced the release of its new viewers, iPIX Java Viewer Lite V3.3 and iPIX RealProducer Plug-in. The RealProducer Plug-in is a completely new product developed to support 180-degree by 180-degree streaming media. Theoretically, this could be used to create more interactive films and Web conferences.

iPIX technology has taken advantage of browser Java support and given users the choice to view iPIX images without a plug-in. The recent Java applet is 40K in size. Users viewing iPIX with these applets see a lower-resolution image than the users with the plug-in.

System Requirements

Operating Systems: Windows 95 or higher, Macintosh iMac
Browsers: Netscape 3.X and higher, Internet Explorer 3.X and higher, Opera and AOL running on Windows.
File Size: 1MB

Internet Explorer 5.5 SP2 and 6.0 and Netscape Navigator 6.X Compatibility

When a user indicates he or she is using Internet Explorer 4.X or higher, iPIX automatically installs an ActiveX version of its plug-in. This version should work with the latest Internet Explorer and SP2. Netscape should work without problems.

PROS AND CONS

iPIX tours are something to see. People who might never have the chance to visit exotic landmarks, famous museums, and interesting exhibits can use the Internet to experience these places virtually. Realtors can upload virtual tours of available properties for potential buyers. iPIX also allows the creator to place "hot spots" in the tours; when a user mouses over part of an image, a text box pops up with further information about that item; the creator can also make links to other Web pages from the hot spot. The ability to turn 360-degrees, any direction, and click on items of interest for more details is, if not the same as being somewhere, at least a good start.

The iPIX plug-in is easy to install and use. The cursor turns into a pointing hand to show in which direction the user will be taken if he or she clicks the mouse. A small blue bull's-eye target appears when a hotspot link is available. A user unfamiliar or uneasy with mouse navigation may need some guidance, as prolonged depression of the mouse may result in rapid spinning around the image.

Being able to see what is left and right of an image has its advantages, but a full 360-degree view includes the ceiling and floor. Sometimes, such as the panoramic tour of the Great Wall of China, this adds to the experience. Often, especially for tours held inside buildings, this is distracting. A beautifully decorated dome or hand-loomed rug can be interesting to look at, but most times the user is looking at fluorescent lights overhead or indoor/outdoor carpeting underfoot (many tours plant an image of their institutional slogan on the floor, which also seems extraneous).

QuickTime's QTVR creates a similar tour to iPIX, but the QT files are larger. QuickTime is an Apple product, which has its own benefits and drawbacks. Not all of the iPIX software works with Macintoshes; QuickTime is an alternative for that platform. On the other hand, Internet Explorer, a Microsoft product, can have difficulties with the QuickTime viewer. When choosing between QTVR and iPIX, consider the environment and audience.

Examples

THE FRICK COLLECTION

www.frick.org

Virtual Tour Tips

Once Inside the Tour:

FOR CLOSE-UP VIEW OF ART:
Double-click on selected art works
(indicated as a link) for a closer
view, descriptive text and a brief
artist's biography.

To Hide/Show Hotspots:

WINDOWS USERS:
Right mouse click in the IPIX
window to display preferences
menu.

MACINTOSH USERS:
Hold down command key
and click in the IPIX window
to display preferences menu.

Figure 3-5. The Frick Collection
Copyright The Frick Collection, New York

The Frick Collection, housed in New York, provides a virtual tour on its Web site using iPIX. Users can see individual rooms and galleries at either full-screen or half-screen size. Hot spots give further information about special art pieces.

THE BUTTERFLY CONSERVATORY

www.amnh.org/exhibitions/butterflies/tour.html

Figure 3-6. The Butterfly Conservatory
Courtesy of the American Museum of Natural History, 2002
The Butterfly Conservatory at the American Museum of Natural History iPIX tour gives users the experience of being inside the vivarium. The Web site invites users to count the butterflies they find in the tour.

360 DEGREE IMAGES OF MONO LAKE

www.spacescience.com/ipix/

Figure 3-7. Mono Lake, California
Scientists believe California's Mono Lake may resemble the dried lake beds of Mars. Discovery Channel's site gives users a panoramic view of the Great Wall of China. Helpfully, the page has links to both Java and iPIX plug-in versions of the tour.

Finding and Installing

Any Java-enabled browser can play an iPIX tour without the iPIX plug-in. The quality is not as high, and the user does not control the view; the panorama automatically revolves around the user.

The plug-in can be installed from the iPIX site at www.ipix.com. The site will ascertain which browser and operating system the user has and send him or her to the correct version of the plug-in. If another version of the plug-in is sought, visit www.ipix.com/download/alternative.html to see a listing of all versions. Drop-down boxes give users the opportunity to match their particular operating system and browser together.

Once the user has clicked on the button marked PROCEED, the plug-in is automatically installed onto the computer. This automatic installer will also check to see if the user already has the iPIX Plug-in and

Viewer on the machine; if so, no files will be added. When the installation is complete, the user will see a box stating that the process was successful.

Troubleshooting

Problem: I am having difficulty viewing an iPIX image.

Solution: First, make sure you have the most current version of the iPIX viewer and plug-in.

If that doesn't fix the problem, look at your browser. Although iPIX claims to work with Netscape and Internet Explorer versions 3.x, best results can be obtained by using the 4.x or higher versions. Upgrading to a newer version of these browsers may solve the problem. If you are using an older version of AOL, upgrade to the 32-bit version.

Finally, if you are using Netscape on a Macintosh computer, try raising the memory allocation for Netscape to at least 9 MB.

Problem: I am using an operating system or browser not compatible with the iPIX Plug-in and Viewer. How can I see iPIX images?

Solution: You can try the previous version of the iPIX Viewer, available at www.ipix.com/download/alternative.html. This viewer will open outside of the browser as a helper application. Alternatively, you can view iPIX images on the Web without the plug-in by choosing to view the lower-quality Java version.

Creating Files

Although a finished iPIX image appears to be 360 degrees by 360 degrees, it is actually created by taking multiple photos with a special fish-eye lens. The resulting 180-degree photos, called hemispheres, are then spliced together with iPIX technology. Any visible seams are rubbed out using Photoshop.

When users buy iPIX products, they are purchasing the tools to create the hemispheres and a limited number of opportunities to turn those hemispheres into 360-degree immersive images. After the photos are taken, the user sends them to the iPIX company, who then melds them together into the resulting image. The finished product is sent back to the user or the Webmaster to post onto the Web site. Each time a photo is sent in to be made into iPIX images, one-conversion opportunity, called a "key," is used. Additional keys beyond the initial purchase can be bought. iPIX offers a number of software "suites" to provide users with the correct programs for their needs.

The camera technology needed to take 180-degree photos can be pricier than the process of turning them into iPIX images. An iPIX-compatible digital camera, a tripod, a rotator, and a fish-eye lens are required.

As of September 2001, the iPIX site was advertising the professional version of its Nikon kit for $2495, but further investigation found starter kits for about $500.

Library Uses

Immersive images are designed for tours, and many museums have created excellent online experiences for users. Libraries with online tours have traditionally used still images, but more are moving to QuickTime and iPIX files.

South Dakota's Rapid City Public Library decided to implement a virtual tour to orient its many one-time, out-of-state visitors who dropped in while traveling to nearby Mount Rushmore. iPIX was chosen over other technologies because of its files' quick downloading, ideal for visitors using modems. Users can go to an alphabetical listing of iPIX views, or visit a Web page containing a static floor plan image with clickable yellow dots to see specific areas of the library. The iPIX tours contain

Figure 3-8. Rapid City Public Library
Mousing over targets leads to further information about different areas of Rapid City Public Library.
Courtesy of the Rapid City Public Library, Web work by Bill Paez of Ace Communications
rcplib.sdln.net/Tour/tourindex.asp.

hot spots that pop up information when moused over. For example, when the user passes the mouse over a desk in the tour, a message is displayed explaining this is the circulation desk and clicking on this link will provide further information about circulation.

The Bernard Becker Library at University of Washington School of Medicine has an iPIX tour of its seven-level building. Unlike the Rapid City library tour in which users can jump from one area to another, the Becker tour is constructed on more linear lines. After viewing an iPIX image, users can choose to see the "next" or "previous" image, or return to the home page. The 360-degree views of the Becker Library provide an interesting look at the atrium connecting the library to the academic school.

Library Atrium   Close Window

Welcome to the Bernard Becker Library at Washington University School of Medicine. Dedicated in 1989, the Becker Library consists of seven levels and is physically connected to the School of Medicine by a glass atrium as shown above from the library entrance.

Figure 3-9. Bernard Becker Library, Washington University School of Medicine Many libraries like Becker provide instructions on navigating iPIX tours for their users.
becker.wustl.edu/information/tour.

MRSID

Purpose

Image files viewed online typically have small dimensions, large file size, and poor resolution. Larger, higher-quality images require long download times and may exceed the dimensions of the browser window or computer monitor and require scrolling to view the entire image.

MrSID, **M**ulti-**r**esolution **S**eamless **I**mage **D**atabase, was created to manage large digital images. First developed by the Los Alamos National Laboratory (LANL), MrSID is based on the technology used to store and retrieve fingerprint images. In 1992, LizardTech was formed as an offshoot of LANL and developed the MrSID technology for commercial applications. MrSID was introduced commercially in 1997.

System Requirements

Processor: 200MHz PC or greater; Apple G3 or greater
Operating Systems: Windows 95 or greater; Mac OS 9 or greater
Installed RAM: 64MB minimum
Browsers: Netscape 4.5-4.7X; Internet Explorer, PC: 4.0 or greater, Mac: 5.0 or greater

Internet Explorer 5.5 SP2 and 6.0 and Netscape 6.X Compatibility

MrSID contains an ActiveX control and is compatible with the most recent versions of Internet Explorer. The current version of MrSID is not compatible with Netscape 6.

Pros and Cons

The biggest benefit of MrSID is its ability to create and display high-quality, high-resolution images in a greatly compressed file. The compression ratio of MrSID files to other image files such as TIFF can be over 20:1. Very little image quality is lost from the original format and the MrSID file can be manipulated by the users in a variety of ways.

Each MrSID file contains multiple resolutions of the image. Users can zoom in on an area of interest, and the file redraws itself so that the selected area is centered and enlarged. When zooming, only the selected and visible area of the file updates so users do not have to wait for the entire image to resize. Users can also pan along the image to move to other areas. When panning and zooming, the MrSID window will momentarily pixelate, but when the image redraws, the image is clear and sharp. Internet Explorer users also have the option of resizing the MrSID viewing area.

Users of MrSID can save the images they are viewing in a variety of formats. The entire file can be saved as a SID file for viewing in the MrSID viewer, or the currently visible portion of the file may be saved in JPG or BMP file format for use in other software.

MrSID's greatest use is in the viewing of online maps. In the past, the only way to obtain high-quality map data was to visit physical map collections. Poorly preserved maps were often not accessible at all. With MrSID technology, those maps can be converted to digital images and viewed, printed, and explored by anyone with access to the Internet. Installing MrSID on public stations in libraries will allow access to these collections.

In addition to maps, the growing popularity of geographic information systems (GIS) and data will also make MrSID a more useful tool. Census information and aerial images of geographical locations can also be viewed with the plug-in.

On the other hand, libraries may be hesitant to add another piece of software to the desktop, especially one that serves a small percentage of the population. Many of the Web sites that offer SID files make the images available in multiple formats. In addition to viewing the files with the MrSID plug-in, many sites offer the ability to view the image with Java or without the plug-in directly in the browser window. Viewing the image without the plug-in limits the functionality of the map. For example, users cannot pan in an image or control the printing output. However, they can usually zoom and resize the image. Libraries that choose not to install the plug-in software should promote the use of the browser or Java viewing options where available.

Examples

REGIONAL TRAILS IN KING COUNTY

www.esri.com/mapmuseum/mapbook_gallery/volume16/tourism1.html

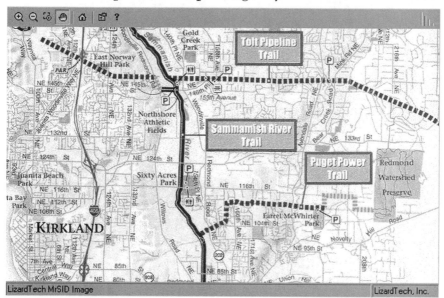

Figure 3-10. Hiking Trails, King County, Washington
Map produced by the King County Parks Division Geographic Information System in cooperation with the King County GIS Center.
The original map shows all of the trails in the area. Zooming in on the hiking map allows viewers to highlight specific trails and the surrounding areas.
Copyright © 2000 King County, Washington

NASA GEOGRAPHIC MAPS OF THE WESTERN UNITED STATES

zulu.ssc.nasa.gov/mrsid/index.pl?category=us_western

Figure 3-11. Northern California Coastline
One region of the Western States map highlights the Northern California coastline.

Figure 3-12. Northern San Francisco
Zooming in on the San Francisco Bay Area region of the map allows the user to zoom in on a high-resolution map of northern San Francisco, the Bay, Treasure Island, Alcatraz, and the Golden Gate Bridge linking San Francisco to Marin.

Finding and Installing

The MrSID plug-in can be found at www.lizardtech.com/download. Users should select the option to download MrSID Browser Plug-in 1.3. Save the install file to the desktop and double-click on the downloaded file to install the program. Choose yes when asked if you wish to make MrSID your default SID viewing software. Users of Netscape will also notice that Netscape will open and MrSID will configure itself as a plug-in.

Troubleshooting

Problem: I am trying to print an image, but the Print Image option in my toolbar is grayed out.

Solution: The administrator of the site that is sending you the image has disabled this feature on the server. You are unable to print the file from the MrSID plug-in; however, you should still be able to print the visible area by using the print function of your browser.

Problem: The image size on my screen is too small. I'd like to resize the image but the option for Frame Size is grayed out.

Solution: Are you using Netscape Navigator? The Frame Size option is only available in Internet Explorer. With the frame size feature enabled, you would be able to change the dimensions of the visible area to any one of four predefined sizes or customize the image size to fit your needs.

Problem: On my PC, the images appear grainy and are oddly colored. What am I doing wrong?

Solution: You probably have your color setting set too low. For optimal viewing, set your colors to 16 bit. To make this change, right mouse click on your Windows desktop, then choose Properties. Select the Setting tab and change the selection in the Colors pull-down menu to High Color (16 bit).

Creating Files

MrSID files are created with other LizardTech software: MrSID Geo and MrSID Photo. MrSID Geo allows users to work with multiple images and stitch them together to create one large image. The resulting image is then compressed to form a workable file. MrSID Photo comes in three versions: Solo, Photoshop, and Workgroup. The Solo version allows personal users to encode their digital images (TIFF and JPG) from digital cameras as MrSID files in order to create smaller files. MrSID Photoshop works as an add-on to Photoshop so that all images can be converted from within Photoshop to MrSID format. The Workgroup version is meant for use with conversion of large amounts of data.

Library Uses

The libraries at the University of Texas at Arlington have created a Web site at libraries.uta.edu/ccon called Cartographic Connections. The collection of historical maps from the 1500s to the 1900s was created with the purpose of making historic maps of Texas and beyond available to secondary-school students and teachers. The maps are searchable and browsable and can be displayed in the browser window, with the MrSID plug-in, or with Java.

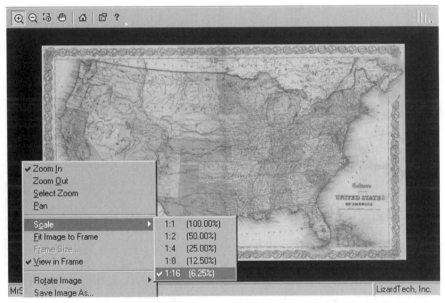

Figure 3-13. J. H. Colton's Map of the United States of America. New York: Johnson & Browning, 1855.

Shown at the smallest available resolution, this view of the files provides an overall image of the map of the United States.

Courtesy, The University of Texas at Arlington Libraries. The Cartographic Connections Web site was made possible, in part, by a grant from the Houston Endowment, Inc.

Figure 3-14. Close-up of Maine on Colton's Map
Zooming in on an area of interest brings the desired information closer. In this case, a portion of Maine is shown at the highest possible resolution: 100%.
Courtesy, The University of Texas at Arlington Libraries.
The Cartographic Connections Web site was made possible, in part, by a grant from the Houston Endowment, Inc.

The American Memory Collection at the Library of Congress, memory.loc.gov, contains many MrSID maps. The Library of Congress was LizardTech's first commercial customer. Searching the American Memory Collection for MrSID digital files produces a list of collections for further exploration.

American Memory Collections: Digital Format: MrSID

To explore an individual collection, click on its title in the list below.
This will reveal more information about the collection and further options for searching and browsing the collection items.

Search For Items In the Collections Listed Below
To remove a collection from your search, click on its checkbox. All collections are checked initially. Collections marked with a ● are not searchable.

| | SEARCH | [Search Tips] |

Match any of these words ▾ Include word variants (e.g. plurals) ▾

Return a maximum of 500 bibliographic records.
* What American Memory resources are included in this search?

Collection list: by Keyword | by Title   Show descriptions

☑ **African-American Odyssey ~ Exhibit ~ Multiformat**
    Title: African American Odyssey

☑ **Civil War Maps ~ 1861-1865**
    Title: Civil War Maps

☑ **Folk Culture, Florida ~ Multiformat ~ 1937-1942**
    Title: Florida Folklife from the WPA Collections, 1937-1942

☑ **Liberia ~ Maps ~ 1830-1870**
    Title: Maps of Liberia, 1830-1870

☑ **Maps ~ 1500-1999**
    Title: Map Collections: 1544-1999

☑ **National Parks ~ Maps**
    Title: Mapping the National Parks

☑ **Panoramic Maps ~ 1847-1929**
    Title: Panoramic Maps

Figure 3-15. MrSID Documents in the Library of Congress's American Memory Collection

WHIP!/VOLO VIEW EXPRESS

Purpose

Computer-aided drafting (CAD) programs are used in a variety of industries including architecture; civil, electrical, and mechanical engineering; construction; manufacturing; building and landscape design; and mapping and geographic information. Autodesk's AutoCAD is the industry leader in CAD software packages. CAD software is costly and useful only to those who need to create and manipulate technical drawings. However, professionals in these industries wanted a method of sharing drawings with each other in a read-only version that did not require the viewer to own the AutoCAD software. With AutoCAD Release 14 the

Drawing Web Format (DWF) was introduced, allowing users to create smaller files that could be shared with non-AutoCAD users over the Web. Conversion of DWG (the standard AutoCAD drawing format) files to DWF removes non-essential, non-visual information from the file and compresses it to make file sharing faster and easier.

The two free programs Autodesk provides for the viewing of DWF files are Whip! and Volo View Express. Whip! is a plug-in and is the older of the two programs. Although it was specifically designed to read DWF files, the newer versions of AutoCAD produce DWF files that Whip! is unable to read. Volo View Express was recently developed to replace Whip! and can handle more AutoCAD files. However, Volo View is a helper-application and is therefore a less integrated tool for the user. The basic functions of the programs are similar.

System Requirements

VOLO VIEW

Processor:	Pentium PC
Operating Systems:	Windows 98 or greater
Installed RAM:	64MB recommended, 32MB minimum
Browsers:	Internet Explorer 5.01 or greater MUST be installed, Netscape 4.5 or greater (only works if IE5.01 is also installed)
File Size:	25MB

WHIP!

Processor:	486 PC or greater
Operating Systems:	Windows 95 or greater
Installed RAM:	64MB recommended, 32MB minimum
Browsers:	Internet Explorer 3.02 or greater; Netscape 3.01-4.7x
File Size:	3.5MB

INTERNET EXPLORER 5.5 SP2 AND 6.0 AND NETSCAPE NAVIGATOR 6.X COMPATIBILITY

Volo View is fully compatible with the most recent versions of both Internet Explorer and Netscape Navigator. Whip! is incompatible with Netscape 6.

Pros and Cons

Whip! and Volo View Express users can view detailed schematics of manufactured goods, architectural sites, maps, and more. Viewers can pan within the drafted images and zoom in on areas of interest. The

Zoom Rectangle tool allows users to define the perimeter of the area to zoom. Files that are built with layers have options for viewing the drawings with selected layers turned off. This is particularly useful when viewing complex diagrams. Finally, both programs have the ability to print and to save DWF files in DWF, DWG, or BMP format. Volo View's menus appear at the top of the helper application; Whip! users should right-mouse-click to activate the menu option.

As with all of the tools in this chapter, Whip! and Volo View Express have a limited audience. Libraries will have to weigh the usefulness of this tool to their specific user group against the computer resources and staffing needed to install, support, and maintain the software. The biggest drawback of the programs is that they are both Windows-only tools. Currently, Autodesk does not support the Macintosh or Unix platforms.

Examples

MONTANA STATE UNIVERSITY, BOZEMAN CAMPUS MAP—REID HALL

www.facilities.montana.edu/map/campus.asp

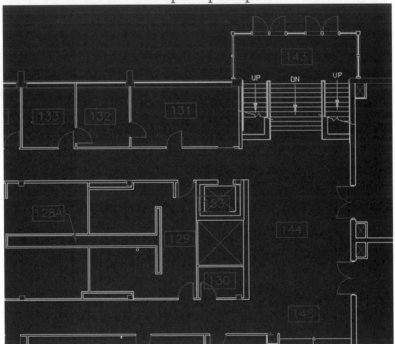

Figure 3-16. Reid Hall. Montana State University Bozeman
The Office of Facilities Services at MSU Bozeman provides interactive AutoCAD maps of the campus buildings that allow viewers to display floor plans, zoom in on specific rooms, pan, and turn layers (such as interior walls, exterior walls, windows, doors, and elevators, etc.) on and off.

GLACIER BAY MARINE PRODUCTS—MARK II COMPRESSOR UNIT

www.glacierbay.com/fileview.htm

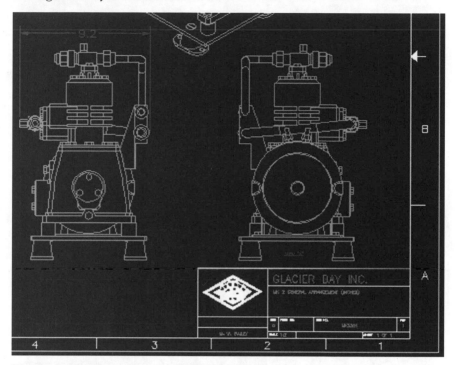

Figure 3-17. Glacier Bay Compression Unit

Glacier Bay Marine Products have made their product library available in a variety of formats including 2D CAD drawings of this compressor unit. The graphics show line drawing schematics for each unit from all sides and include measurements to indicate size.

By permission of Glacier Bay, Inc. Not for reproduction.

SOUTHERN ILLINOIS UNIVERSITY EDWARDSVILLE—TOPOGRAPHIC MAP

www.siue.edu/UNIVERSITYPARK/topoview.htm

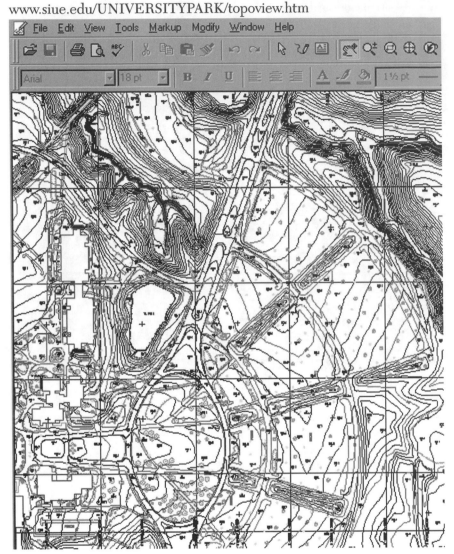

Figure 3-18. Southern Illinois University Edwardsville's Topographic Map
Southern Illinois University Edwardsville's topographic map includes elevation of the entire campus, indicates landscape features such as water and trees, and provides locations of buildings and parking structures. Viewers can zoom and pan to get a closer view of specific areas.
Courtesy of University Park, Southern Illinois University Edwardsville, Inc.

Finding and Installing

Whip! and Volo View Express can be downloaded from the Autodesk Web site at www.autodesk.com in the Products and Services section.

The Volo View page offers users options when downloading: the full current version, earlier versions, and a smaller version that reads only DWF files (not DWG). During installation, Volo View will not detect the browsers installed on the system. After installation, the first time a link to an AutoCAD file is selected, the user will need to configure the browser to associate the file type with the Volo View software.

During the Whip! install for Netscape and Internet Explorer version 5.5 SP1 and below, a Java Security box will ask the user to grant permission to install software on the system. Whip! will automatically detect the installed browsers and configure itself as the default viewer for AutoCAD files. Restarting the browser will complete the installation. When downloading Whip! from within IE6, AutoCAD will automatically send the user to the ActiveX control version of Whip!. Users must agree to download the program by clicking Yes on the Security Warning pop-up box. When the installation is complete, a DWF file will appear in the browser window.

Troubleshooting

Problem: I want to change the scale of my image before printing.

Solution: In Whip!, there are no printing options. You can print using the browser's print function, which will print the entire Web page, or use the right mouse button to active Whip!-specific functions. Printing from the resulting pop-up menu allows you to print the DWF file only. In Volo View, print options can be set under the File menu by selecting Page Setup. Although you can change some settings such as the drawing units and the margins, the option for scale is grayed out. Printing to scale requires the full version of Volo View; it is not an option in Volo View Express.

Problem: I have both Whip! and Volo View installed because I use multiple browsers. Sometimes a file I view on the Web opens in Whip!, but I'd like to use the more advanced features in Volo View. When that occurs, how can I view the file in Volo View?

Solution: You have two options. For the first, allow Whip! to open the file. Then right click on the file in Whip! and choose the Save As option. Save the file to your local machine, open Volo View and then open the saved file. Another option is to right mouse click on the link to the file (Macintosh users, hold the mouse button down for a few seconds) and choose save link as (Netscape) or Save Target As (Internet Explorer) to save the file to your computer, then open the file in Volo View.

Creating Files

Web formatted DWF files are created by conversion of existing AutoCAD DWG files. Creation of DWF files requires AutoCAD Release 14, AutoCAD 2000 or 2000i, or AutoCAD 2002. The Internet Utilities feature must also be installed. The most basic conversion is the DWFOut feature that saves the open DWG file to DWF. It is also possible to create hyperlinks within the DWF file. URLs can be associated with regions of the file or objects in the file.

When creating DWF files, users have the option of compressing the file. Compression is recommended if Internet connection speed is a concern. There is also an option for selecting the level of precision: low, medium, or high. The higher the precision, the bigger the file, which will also affect download time.

Libraries that would like to make plans of remodeling or building projects available on their Web sites should ask their architects to provide them with DWF files to upload on the library's Web server.

Library Uses

Most academic libraries including colleges and universities as well as community and technical colleges support programs in fields that use CAD drawings. However, there are uses for the general public as well. For example, Chilton's auto repair guides are available in most public libraries. They provide diagrams and instructions for repair of most foreign and domestic makes and models of automobiles. Chilton guides are also available on the Web through a subscription database at www.chiltonpro.com. The technical diagrams in the database are provided in DWF format and Chilton includes the Get Whip! icon on its Web page.

The Hudson Library & Historical Society of Hudson, Ohio has provided a link on their Web site, www.hudson.lib.oh.us, to a presentation about their new building project. Included in the presentation is a link to the floor plans of the new facility. Viewing the plans in Whip! allows visitors to their Web site the opportunity to explore their new library. In addition to outlining the physical footprint of the building and the outlying property, the plans also label service areas and provide layers that define the content of the building. By viewing the layers of the document, users can turn off and on locations such as bookstacks, equipment, shelves, furniture, and lighting to see where these items will be located in the new facility. The "appliance" button even toggles the view of the refrigerator in the kitchen area on and off.

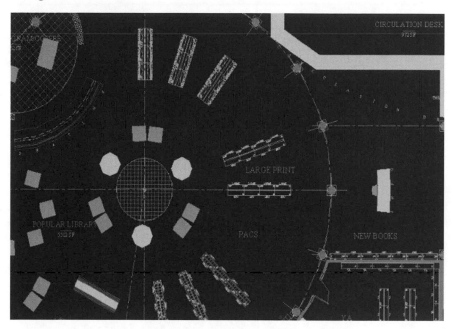

Figure 3-19. Hudson Library & Historical Society Floor Plan
Credits: Dan Meehan & Associates/Hudson Library & Historical Society. Site designed by Jolyn A. Taylor.

Chapter 4

Multimedia Tools

OVERVIEW

Left on their own, Web browsers are rather static, displaying text and unmoving images. Animated GIFS, Java applets, and Javascript enliven things a bit, but for a true multimedia experience, users must turn to media players. The tools in this chapter allow users to listen to music, watch movie clips, and take part in interactive games. Macromedia's Shockwave, Apple's QuickTime, RealOne, Microsoft's Windows Media Player, and Nullsoft's WinAMP are all players designed to provide users with these opportunities.

QuickTime, Real, Windows Media Player, and WinAMP are competitors in the great multimedia players' war. Shockwave is different in that it is designed to play only Macromedia files and does not concern itself with other formats. The other four do not concern themselves with Shockwave, but the struggle amongst them can be ugly. As new versions are released, the differences between them are getting smaller and smaller. This chart compares the four.

	QuickTime 5	RealOne	Windows Media Player 7/7.1	WinAMP 2.7
Creator	Apple	Real	Microsoft	Nullsoft (owned by AOL)
Windows OS	Windows 95+	Windows 98+	Windows 98+	Windows 95+
Mac OS	7.5.5+	No	No	8.5+
Compatible with latest browsers?	Yes (must install ActiveX for IE)	Yes	Yes	Yes
Program size	9.4 MB	21.3 MB	21.4 MB	1.1 MB
Proprietary file format	.MOV	.RA, .RV, .RM	.WMA	none
Plays others' proprietary format?	No	Limited support	No	Yes, if plug-in components installed
Visualizations	Some	Some	Lots	Even more
Cost	Free version; Pro version $29.95	Free version; Pro version $9/month subscription	Free version	Free version
Best uses	Movie trailers	Older streaming video	New streaming video and audio	Audio
Noteworthy	QVTR virtual tours	Many files on the Web are in Real format	Bundled with Windows XP	Active community of users

QUICKTIME

Purpose

Apple's QuickTime software is a multimedia player that supports multi-platform industry-standard multimedia architecture. It delivers synchronized graphics, sound, video, text, and music to the desktop and is primarily used to play movies or other media clips. QuickTime version 5 has standard playback controls including play, pause, fast-forward, rewind, volume control, and playback time stamping.

First introduced in 1991 as a Macintosh program, QuickTime Player quickly became a popular tool for displaying multimedia. Subsequent versions have added support for the Windows operating systems and the ability to handle many more file types. Currently, over 200 audio, video, and sound file types are supported by QuickTime.

QuickTime 5 is actually a suite of programs: QuickTime Player for movies and streaming video, PictureViewer for still images, and the QuickTime Plug-in, which allows for inline viewing of multimedia files in the browser window. Additionally, viewers can manipulate 360-degree virtual reality (VR) environments with QuickTime Cubic VR.

QuickTime Pro is also available and adds the capability to author QuickTime files in addition to splicing or otherwise editing existing files.

System Requirements

Processor:	Pentium-based or compatible PC; PowerPC-based Macintosh
Operating Systems:	Windows 95 or later; Mac OS 7.5.5 or later
Installed RAM:	At least 32 MB
Browsers:	Netscape 3.X or greater, Microsoft Internet Explorer 3.X or greater, AOL 3.0 or greater
File Size:	9.4 MB (QT Player, browser plug-ins, VR support)

Internet Explorer 5.5 SP2 and 6.0 and Netscape 6.X Compatibility

QuickTime and QuickTime VR are compatible with Internet Explorer 6. After installing IE6, users should visit the QuickTime homepage at www.apple.com/quicktime. Apple will detect that the ActiveX control is needed and will prompt users to download and install it. After the installation is complete, all of the QuickTime features will be available. There are no known conflicts with Netscape 6.X.

Pros and Cons

Since QuickTime has traditionally been used to view movie trailer clips, libraries may consider the software to be a frivolous addition to the desktop. In reality, current generation multimedia files encompass a much larger scope of coverage. For example, multimedia can be used to teach manual tasks such as sign language or CPR; display video (television, motion picture); tour distant lands, historical sites, or college campuses; or teach a surgical procedure.

One of the nicest features of QuickTime is the fact that it supports so many file types. This one piece of software could supplant many others currently used for any of the following tasks (and more!): viewing graphic files including BMP, Photoshop, TIFF, and PICT; playing audio files in AU, AIFF, WAV, MP3, and MIDI; displaying videos and animation in MPEG, AVI, and MOV.

QuickTime requires relatively powerful machines with lots of RAM. Media running on slower machines or those with inadequate memory will tend to pause and skip during playback. Version 5 has an added feature, called Skip Protection that smoothes out streaming video to combat the pause and skip tendencies of slow or unstable Internet connections.

The multimedia files played by QuickTime are typically large in size and either require a fair amount of storage space on the local machine or a lot of bandwidth to play over the Web.

Examples

MOVING SAFELY ACROSS AMERICA

safety.fhwa.dot.gov/fourthlevel/msaa

Figure 4-1. Moving Safely Across America Video
The Federal Highway Administration, U.S. Department of Transportation has created an interactive Web site dedicated to safety on the road. The Educators section contains many QuickTime movies on topics from road conditions, to road hazards, to rules of the road. The video pictured above highlights the importance of roadside "crash cushions."

NOBEL E-MUSEUM

www.nobel.se/help/plugins/quicktime.html

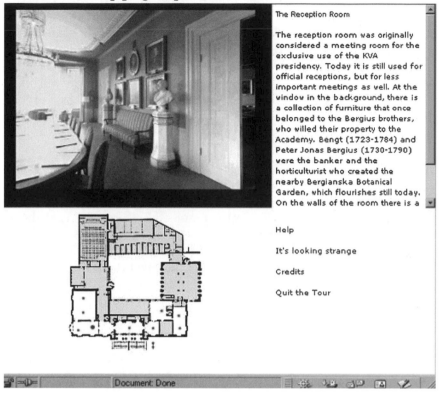

Figure 4-2. Royal Swedish Academy of Science Virtual Tour
Take a virtual tour of the Royal Swedish Academy of Sciences with QuickTime VR. The map at the bottom of the window shows in blue the areas of the museum that can be viewed in the round. Using the mouse, the user can rotate around the room and select "hot spots" to move from one room to the next. Copyright © 2001 The Nobel Foundation

Finding and Installing

The software is available in two versions: QuickTime, which is free, and QuickTime Pro, which costs $29.95. The pro version is geared towards media production and provides tools to edit, crop, resize, convert file formats, add special effects, and compress files.

The software can be downloaded from Apple Computer's Web site at www.apple.com/quicktime. The professional version is highlighted; the free version is more difficult to find. Two download options are available. The QuickTime Installer downloads a small program that allows the user to download and install the entire program directly from the Web. Those behind firewalls or without cookies enabled may not be able to use the Web installer. The Stand-alone Installer allows the user to download the entire file to the local machine and perform a local install. This version needs to be unzipped before it can be installed.

During installation, QuickTime will prompt the user to select file types that QuickTime should run. Standard QuickTime installation will run most movie and sound files, and many still picture types. For other files (for example, MPEG, BMP, GIF, JPG, WAV, AVI), file type handling can be selected to extend QuickTime's power.

Troubleshooting

Problem: QuickTime streaming doesn't work. My computer is located behind a firewall.

Solution: PC—from the Edit menu, select Preferences, and then Streaming Transport. Mac—from the Settings Control Panel select Streaming Transport. Both—select Auto Configure. QuickTime will attempt to receive any streaming files using the Hypertext Transfer Protocol (HTTP) instead of Real Time Streaming Protocol (RTSP), which is often blocked by firewalls.

Problem: I can't save movies from my QuickTime browser plug-in.

Solution: Upgrade to QuickTime Pro. The standard version will play files but not allow you to save.

Problem: I'm watching a movie in my Web browser and the video keeps stopping and starting during playback.

Solution: PC—from the Edit menu, select Preferences, and then Connection Speed. Mac—from the Settings Control Panel select Connection Speed. Both—select the appropriate connection speed. Since QuickTime starts playing files before the file has completely downloaded, selecting a faster speed than your actual connection will cause the program to stop playback while waiting for the rest of the file to download.

Creating Files

QT

Starting with a digital video file (either created with a digital video recorder or by capturing an analog file onto a computer and digitizing), QuickTime Pro allows media developers to divide the file into tracks, compress the file, add text such as subtitles, and include interactivity including hypertext links, Flash components, Java applets, and pop-up menus. The file can then be saved into a QT file with the Fast Start feature. Fast Start allows Web browsers to start playing the beginning of a QuickTime file while the file is still downloading on the user's computer.

Fast Start delivery works on a regular HTTP server; no streaming server is required.

VR

QuickTime VR files are created using programs specifically designed to create either panoramic views or rotating object views. Two popular VR creation tools are QuickTime VR Authoring Studio (Mac only, $395) and VR Toolbox (Mac or PC, $300). These programs use still photos or videos to piece together seamless 360-degree views. Creators can use the software to create "hot spot" that allows users to "move" through the environment, jumping from one viewpoint to another.

Library Uses

The most popular use for QuickTime in libraries is a library tour. Some libraries offer QuickTime VR tours that allow users to virtually "walk" through the library. Various library resource and service areas are highlighted and text accompanies the images. However, few of these tours are narrated or include "hot spots" that allow the viewer to jump from one area to another. The University of Rochester Medical Center Miner Library provides a tour that links not only to other rooms or areas within the library, but also to Web pages that highlight the resources and services for each area. To view the tour, visit www.urmc.rochester.edu/Miner/QTVRTour/LibTour.html.

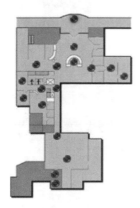

Welcome to the Edward G. Miner Library.

Figure 4-3. Edward G. Miner Library Virtual Tour
The floor plan on the left provides a key to each of the areas available in the tour. Clicking on the red areas will take users to that portion of the tour. In the QTVR tour on the left, hotspots are described in text at the bottom of the video screen.
Copyright © University of Rochester Medical Center, 1999-2002.

Other libraries have created QuickTime movie tours that are narrated, guided tours through the library. The Pollak Library at California State University, Fullerton has created a production-quality tour complete with hosts and a soundtrack. Each portion of the tour includes an optional "Read Script" choice that displays the text of the tour, complete with definitions of unfamiliar terms—including colloquialisms and slang—as an aid for English as a second language students. A multiple-choice quiz accompanies each portion of the tour. This tour is one of the most professional library tours on the Web and can be seen at www.library. fullerton.edu/tour.

Figure 4-4. CSUF Pollak Library Video Tour
Courtesy of John Hickok, Audiovisual Librarian, California State University, Fullerton, jhickok@fullerton.edu

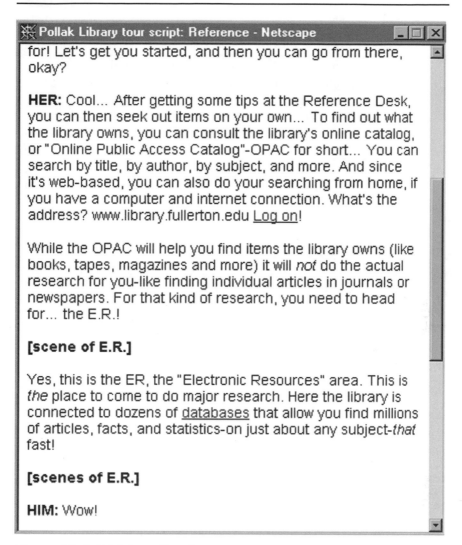

Figure 4-5. Pollak Library Tour Script
Courtesy of John Hickok, Audiovisual Librarian, California State University, Fullerton, jhickok@fullerton.edu

SHOCKWAVE

Purpose

Macromedia's Shockwave player allows for the viewing of multimedia files like interactive games, product simulations, and video clips. It plays back sound, video, animation, and responds to mouse clicks by the user. Introduced in late 1995, Shockwave was a plug-in devised to make

Macromedia's Director content, intended for offline use such as inter-active CD-ROMs, Web-viewable.

Macromedia acquired the Futuresplash company, which had a Web animation creation program and a player capable of downloading and playing these files in the browser. Renamed Flash, the program creates small files that are quickly downloaded and do not become distorted when magnified. Flash is built for online interactivity, making it an alternative to Javascript.

Until recently, users needed two plug-ins from Macromedia: Shockwave Director Player and Shockwave Flash Player. Thankfully, with version 8 Macromedia bundled the two together into one Shockwave Player.

System Requirements

Processor: Pentium II or higher
Operating Systems: Windows 95 or higher; Mac OS 8.1
Installed RAM: 32 MB
Browsers: Netscape 4.X and higher (although not 6.0); Internet
                      Explorer 4.X and higher
File Size: 3400K

Internet Explorer 5.5SP2 and 6.0 and Netscape 6.X Compatibility

Shockwave should work without problem in the most recent Internet Explorer versions. Netscape 6.0 does not support Shockwave, but versions 6.1 and later do.

Pros and Cons

Many libraries are concerned that the viewing of multimedia files will take up too much bandwidth. Shockwave files are smaller, on average, than RealOne or QuickTime files. Another advantage of Shockwave is its bundling of its media, meaning a piece can begin playing while the remainder is being downloaded. Of course, the size of a Shockwave file depends on its creator; some files may hog bandwidth. A fast connection and a good computer are needed to make Shockwave viable.

The computer must run Windows or Mac OS; browsers must be recent Netscape, Internet Explorer, or AOL versions. Currently, Shockwave does not work with Netscape 6.0, or on a UNIX platform.

Some libraries might be hesitant to install Shockwave on their machines because it is thought of as a purely entertainment-driven plug-in. Many of the Shockwave pieces on the Web are games, cartoons, and movies. Having the Shockwave plug-in will give users access to these sites, which may not be the library's mission. But the same unparalleled interaction between the user and the file that makes Shockwave optimal for leisure pursuits also make it ideal for training and simulation exercises. The following examples show the technology that can be used for educational purposes.

Examples

Dr. Disguise

www.cia.gov/ciakids/spyguy/disguise.html

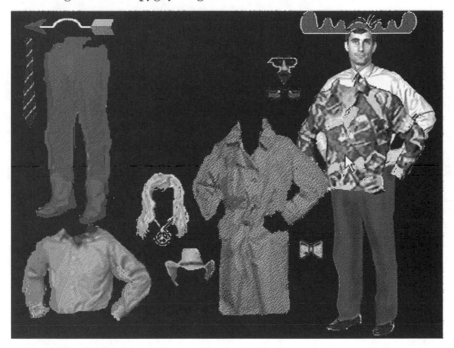

Figure 4-6. Central Intelligence Agency Kids' Page
In this Shockwave piece, users drag clothing and disguises onto the CIA spy.

BOUYANCY

www.brainpop.com/science/forces/buoyancy

Figure 4-7. BrainPop's Buoyancy Movie
Brainpop animated characters Tim and Moby explain the mystery of buoyancy to children. Users can pause, fast-forward, rewind, play, or stop these brightly colored cartoons with the small buttons in the lower right-hand corner of the screen.
Copyright © Brainpop

ENDNOTE TUTORIAL

www.endnote.com/support/en4tutorial.asp

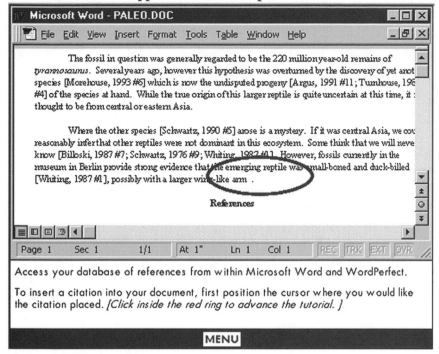

Figure 4-8. Endnote Tutorial
Endnote provides a Shockwave tutorial showing how to use its bibliographic management software. The use of Shockwave allows for greater interaction than many online tutorials.

Finding and Installing

The Shockwave player is bundled into most browsers, but users will probably need to upgrade their version. They can install the player for free from the Macromedia site at www.macromedia.com/downloads. The site includes clear installation instructions. Since users need to quit their browser before installing the plug-in, they should be sure to print out the directions beforehand.

Shockwave distributes a stand-alone installer to the computer; each computer station will need to be loaded with the plug-in individually.

When users visit a site requiring Shockwave and do not yet have it, they will be prompted to download the player. Dialog boxes will ask for age, name, and e-mail contact information; a generated Welcome message will be sent to the address provided. This welcome message includes a link allowing users to opt out of promotional e-mail from Macromedia. Because the plug-in will be automatically "pushed" to the computer as soon as someone accesses a site using Shockwave, the plug-in should be installed ahead of time.

Troubleshooting

Problem: I recently installed the latest version of Shockwave and am now having problems.

Solution: Shockwave is bundled with most browsers and many operating systems. Sometimes this earlier version is corrupt in some way, and when you try and replace it with the new version, the upgrade may not work. You must uninstall the old Shockwave Director and Flash players. The uninstaller for Shockwave Director can be downloaded by following the Macromedia link to Troubleshooting Shockwave at www.macromedia.com/support/shockwave.

You can uninstall Flash by deleting the file. Flash is housed in different places, depending upon your operating system:

WINDOWS 95/98

Delete the swflash.ocx file in the Macromed directory:
C:\WINDOWS\SYSTEM\Macromed\flash\

WINDOWS NT

Delete the swflash.ocx file in the Macromed directory:
C:\Windows\System32\Macromed\

NETSCAPE FOR WINDOWS

Delete the NPSWF32.dll file in the Netscape plugins directory:
C:\Program Files\Netscape\Communicator\Program\Plugins

MAC OS

Delete the Shockwave Flash NP-PPC file in the plug-ins folder of your Internet browser.

Problem: My player is not working with Netscape 6.0.

Solution: Upgrade to Netscape 6.1 or higher.

Problem: When I try to install the player with Internet Explorer, I do not get the dialog boxes guiding me through the installation.

Solution: At some point in the past, you may have indicated in a dialog box that you did not want the Macromedia Web players. On the Macromedia site, there are links to executables you can run to free you to install the player.

Creating Files

Macromedia's Director 8.5 Shockwave Studio uses a language known as Lingo to create files. As mentioned before, Director was intended for CD-ROM content, but the company has recognized that Director-files could reach a much wider audience via the Web. The newest version of Director has extended its Web capabilities immensely, adding XML capabilities and multiserver support. Shockwave movies created for the Web in Director are cross-platform compatible, unlike the CD-ROM content. Director's relatively high cost (about $1200) may limit library purchase.

Macromedia's Flash 5 is used mainly to create low-bandwidth animations. You can edit Adobe Illustrator and Macromedia Freehand files in the Flash program. It appears that Macromedia is promoting Flash as an alternative to Adobe Acrobat for creating files that can print cleanly off the browser. Flash's relatively low price ($399) may make it a more attractive purchase for libraries who wish to explore multimedia creation without committing large amounts of money.

Library Uses

Shockwave allows for more interaction between a user and a site. For libraries that design or create Web tutorials this may be of great use. At the University of Texas at Austin, the Digital Information Literacy Office used Director to create Shockwave movies for its information literacy tutorial, TILT.

One example of Shockwave in TILT is the TILTOMETER, a quiz-giving device that responds automatically to the user's answer. When the user clicks on his or her choice, the answer scale oscillates back and forth between red (wrong), yellow (not completely wrong or right), and green (right) bars before settling into one of the bars, revealing the accuracy of the choice, accompanied by a sound clip. When one question is answered correctly, the next query appears automatically.

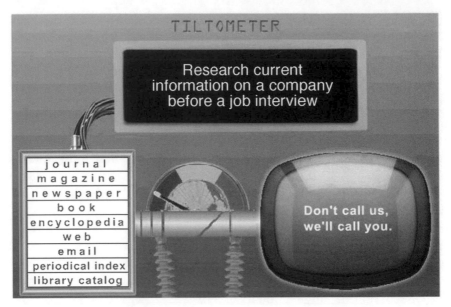

Figure 4-9. Tiltometer Quiz
This user incorrectly answered "journal"; the tutorial ranks the answer in the "red" and takes a humorous approach to informing the user that he or she is wrong.
Permission granted on behalf of the University of Texas System Digital Library, by the Digital Information Literacy Office
tilt.lib.utsystem.edu.

Kings College, London has used Flash to develop a series of animated tutorials for library research. Entitled Cartoon Images for Network Education (CINE), the animations teach how to use Boolean operators, secrets of World Wide Web searching, and ways to use Z39.50.

Libraries should carefully consider their audiences before implementing Shockwave into their sites. The resulting files do not look like HTML-coded Web pages. Text can be slightly fuzzy, and hyperlinks are not clearly marked. Many Web users may be confused or unable to find links.

Creating Shockwave files is a time and skill-intensive task. The library at Kings College, London, worked with computer applications professionals to create the Flash tutorials. At the University of Texas, the library turned to professional programmers and in-house technology staff to complete the multimedia components. Shockwave and Flash provide the highest level of interactive content for the Web, but using these products may be beyond the scope of most libraries' resources.

REALONE

Purpose

One of the oldest and perhaps best-known multimedia players is offered by RealNetworks. Formerly known as RealPlayer, RealOne includes an all-purpose media player and an attached Web browser powered by Internet Explorer. This combination allows the user to view videos and streaming media, listen to music off of the Internet or CDs, and more easily download material from the Web. Although the attached browser and play list features may be of limited interest to the average Web user, the player is one of the key plug-ins for Web surfing. General consensus is that Real has the majority of the player market, although Microsoft's Windows Media Player is making headway.

RealOne supports the native Real formats: RA, RV, RAM for RealVideo and Audio; RT for RealText; and RP for RealPix, which gives access to graphics. The Real formats are generally intended for streaming files. Streaming media can be played while being downloaded, unlike conventional files that cannot be viewed until fully downloaded. This is particularly useful for large files such as video that normally take a long time to download completely.

RealOne can be used to open PNG, JPG, and GIF images, MP3, WAV, and MIDI audio files, and SMIL and MPEG for videos with sound. It offers limited access to Microsoft's proprietary formats, including sound file types AIFF and AVI, and streaming video ASF. Starting with RealOne, WMA is supported.

Users can download the player for RealOne without cost; to access Real's video and music files, they must subscribe to the RealOne service. This service was set up by some of the major record labels which have been searching for a way to provide music online. Subscriptions to either the videos or the music can be had for $9.95 a month; Gold Service members can have both for $19.95 a month. The money allows users to "rent" each file for 30 days.

System Requirements

Processor:	300 MHz Pentium
Operating Systems:	Windows 98 or later; incompatible with Mac. Mac users can use RealPlayer 8.
Installed RAM:	64 MB
Browsers:	Netscape 4.X or greater, Internet Explorer 4.X or greater
File Size:	21.3 MB

Internet Explorer 5.5SP2 and 6.0 and Netscape 6.X Compatibility

RealOne should work with the latest versions of Internet Explorer. It does not work as well with Netscape 6.0. Netscape users should remain with version 4.X, or upgrade to 6.1 or 6.2.

Pros and Cons

Real's advantage is its seniority; it has long been the premiere player for streaming video on the Web and many sites use the Real format for video and audio. Since Windows Media Player (WMP) does not support this format, it is important that libraries that wish to provide access to multimedia on the Web provide RealOne. Until this latest version, Real did not support the Windows Media format.

Real's days as primary player may be numbered however; many of the sites that have Real format are now offering the Windows Media format as an alternative. In a side-by-side comparison with WMP, Real's video and audio quality suffer. The streaming video seems labored, the image edges blur, while the sound is not as sharp as in WMP.

The player itself is fairly straightforward. The newest interface has a softer, more streamlined, almost Macintosh look to it. It resembles Apple's QuickTime quite a bit. The play/pause and stop keys are at the bottom of the screen; users can control the size of the video with a dropdown menu; special "channels" of programming and music can be accessed via the attached browser. The Real player can be viewed in different sizes, from full-screen to a minimal toolbar size. Quality suffers as the picture is increased, however.

The player is the first to integrate so well with the Web. Normally, a video could only be seen within the browser if the page's creator embedded the file in the HTML. With RealOne, the attached browser works in a similar way as if the file were embedded. One could even surf the Web and still see the player. Although this seems like a promising concept, it has not yet reached its potential.

Real is a company trying to make money, and it takes advantage of every opportunity to guide users towards its pay-per-view products. While users may understand this need, they may also become annoyed by Real's attempts. The Real site has useful information about its free player and technical support but finding these pages among the advertisements for the RealOne Service is dishearteningly difficult. Real is also particularly bad about implying that certain features are available to users, only to reveal later that new components must be downloaded or purchased.

RealOne is closely integrated with online viewing; two very unpopular features have arisen from this Internet connection. The first is Real's insistence that whenever someone wants to use the player, he must login, providing the e-mail address and password given when downloading the player. Users must accept Real cookies in order to bypass this login step.

Secondly, RealOne will constantly send "important messages" from its Message Center. This notification will pop-up on a user's screen constantly when RealOne is open. Of course, these messages are advertisements. Earlier versions of Real player allowed users to indicate they did not want to receive e-mail notifications from the company during installation of the player. This newest release does not allow people to opt out unless they visit the Real site and find the correct page. It is bad enough that users must make an extra effort to not receive e-mail from Real; the Message Center just adds insult.

Real has been one of the more controversial plug-ins for libraries. Numerous libraries have shied away from installing it because of its reputation as a bandwidth hog; librarians fear that one person playing Real files could drag down the speed of the entire network. More commonly, though, Real has been problematic in its monopolization of individual computers. It is notorious for installing files throughout the system, and for re-installing previously deleted shortcut icons in the systray and the quick launch bar. If Real is left running in the background, it can slow down the machine noticeably, causing games and other programs to stall or crash.

RealOne was released at the end of 2001 and was a big change from its earlier incarnations. Formerly, Real tried to persuade users to purchase a bigger and better player on which to play files; now, it is giving everyone the same player and urging people to pay for the files themselves. Whether this will succeed is questionable; ten to twenty dollars a month for files that expire after 30 days is not much of a draw to people who are used to Napster and its ilk.

RealOne's newness may also explain its relative instability. Many users have complained that it seems to crash or freeze their computers and other programs more than RealPlayer 8 did. Furthermore, some Real media files that run without trouble in RealPlayer 8 do not work in RealOne. Obviously, this latest player has its share of growing pains.

Examples

NATIONAL FIRE PLANS: FUEL REDUCTION IN MONTANA

www.fireplan.gov/main_features.cfm

Figure 4-10. Fire Risk in Montana Video
This four-minute video discusses how the growth of underbrush and fir trees
has increased the fire risks in Montana. The narrator describes how federal fire
plan money will be used to remove the fir trees in order to spare the Ponde-
rosa Pines.

THE BISBEE DEPORTATION OF 1917: A MANAGEMENT-LABOR CONFLICT IN ARIZONA

digital.library.arizona.edu/bisbee/

Figure 4-11. The Bisbee Deportation of 1917 Video
This approximately 10-minute long RealMedia film, created by Sharlene Grant and Jacob Case, showcases archival photos detailing a copper mining company's deportation of over 1,000 miners suspected of pro-labor sentiments. This example shows RealPlayer in its "compact" viewing mode.
Permission granted by creators Jacob Case and Sharlene Grant

HARVARD UNIVERSITY INSTITUTE OF POLITICS: FORUM ARCHIVES

www.ksg.harvard.edu/iop/forum-archives.html

Figure 4-12. Harvard University, Institute of Politics. 2002.
www.iop.harvard.edu.
Harvard's Kennedy School of Government presents recent Forum events online, such as this speech given by Katherine Harris, Florida Secretary of State. The Forum Web site provides these videos in streaming media format, accessible with Real players.
Cambridge, MA: The Institute of Politics.

Finding and Installing

RealOne can be downloaded for free from its Web site, www.real.com. The Real homepage is redesigned frequently, but one thing remains constant: finding the link to the free player is a challenge. The obvious links to downloadable products are reserved for the pay-for services offered by Real. In February 2002, the link to the free player was at the bottom of the homepage; clicking on it led to a page emphasizing an advertisement for the RealOne Service; the link for the free player is nearby. Do not click on the link for RealOne Trial, as this will sign the user up for a limited trial of the service.

Users must first become "members" of Real before downloading the player. An e-mail address and password are required, and that information serves as a login whenever RealOne is launched. There is a checkbox to allow a cookie to be set to remember that login e-mail and password. Next, the user is brought to a page and asked to choose a site from which to download the player. While the file is being downloaded, a minibrowser will appear showing Real advertisements. This distracting device makes it appear that the user must do something to allow the downloading, but no action is needed.

Once the file is on the desktop, clicking on its icon will begin the installation. The user may choose either "express" or "custom" installation. A wizard will walk the user through the rest of the process.

In this process, the user can automatically set Real.com to be the browser home page and install Real shortcuts on the desktop and systems tray. Even when users turn down the offers, it is not unusual to see the icons installed anyway. A recent installation of RealOne resulted in icons for the player being added to the systems tray, the quick launch bar, the start menu, and the desktop. An AOL icon was added to the desktop as well. Although the user's original homepage was left intact, bookmarks to Real.com and AOL were added without notification to the Internet Explorer Favorites.

Troubleshooting

Problem: I'm having trouble installing RealOne.

Solution: Make sure you have removed any earlier versions of Real that you have on your system. RealOne cannot exist peacefully with them and may in fact refuse to install if you have them on the computer.

Problem: I don't want to login every time I use RealOne.

Solution: You must set the system to accept Real cookies to avoid signing in every time you want to use the player.

1. From the Tools menu, choose Preferences.
2. Click on Preferences.
3. Open the Connection folder.
4. Click on Internet Settings.
5. Checkmark Enable Cookies.

Problem: The video is playing very slowly and the sound is distorted.

Solution: If Internet traffic is heavy or many users are trying to access the file you are trying to view, streaming media can bog down and become jerky or unable to move at all. Even the fastest connections can have this problem. If the Web seems slow in general, you might try visiting the site another time when there is less "Net congestion." If that is not possible, you can try increasing the buffer size so that more of the file will be downloaded into the memory file before playing back. This should smooth the video and sound playback.

1. From the Tools menu, choose Preferences.
2. Open the Connections folder.
3. Choose Playback Settings.
4. You have two choices in the Buffered play section. The buffer indicates how much of the file should be downloaded before being played. The more that is downloaded, the better the quality of the file. You can increase the number of seconds in the "Buffer at least __ seconds" box. The slower your connection, the higher the number of seconds you should allot for buffering. Only the fastest connections should use Instant Playback, which gets rid of downloading all together.
5. Click OK.

Problem: I am having difficulty accessing streaming media from my school or work.

Solution: One possibility is that your institution is located behind a firewall. Some firewalls allow streaming media to be sent through HTTP but not RTSP (see Creating Files for a brief definition of the two protocols). You can set the player to retrieve files only through HTTP in the following steps:

1. From the Tools menu, choose Preferences.
2. Open Network Transports folder and choose Manually Configure Connection Settings.
3. Click on RTSP settings and uncheck all the boxes EXCEPT Use HTTP only.
4. Click OK.
5. Click on PNA settings and uncheck all the boxes EXCEPT Use HTTP only.
6. Click OK twice.

If that does not work, check with your ISP or system administrator.

Problem: I am viewing a streaming media file on the Web, and I don't see any of the player menus or toolbars besides play, stop, and volume. How can I make adjustments to the player?

Solution: Sometimes video or audio files are played within a Web page rather than in a player launched outside of the browser. Developers may decide to embed a multimedia file within a Web page so as to control the look of the video screen and to eliminate the advertising and other non-essential buttons, creating a cleaner look. Right-clicking with the mouse in the video window provides user access to some of the menu items, including preferences and screen size.

Creating Files

Once video or audio material is digitized, it can be converted into Web-readable formats. RealNetworks offers RealSystem Producer to create Real files. The free Basic version provides the creation of Real Video and Real Audio files, the ability to capture live broadcasts for later play-back, and a feature called SureStream that allows the live sending of information to two target audiences. The pay-for Plus system provides more video editing options, bandwidth designations, and backwards compatibility to RealPlayer 5.0.

Transmitting streaming media can be done two ways: on demand or live. Live, or real-time streaming, sends the video to target audiences as it is filmed. Graduation ceremonies, conferences, and meetings are some types of events that benefit from this type of immediacy. The files for real-time streaming need to be small, so the sound and video quality may suffer. Such live broadcasts are sent using Real Time Streaming Protocol (RTSP) and must be housed on a server with special software to support this protocol. Real offers a free, very basic software package for RTSP.

On demand, also known as progressive, streaming media are files that reside on a server waiting to be requested. The user is not expecting to interact with people at the other end of the transmission, so the video can be viewed at his or her convenience. Movie trailers, home movies, and commercials are some types of entertainment that work well with progressive streaming. The files are larger, so the sound and picture are of a better quality, but they can easily become too large for modem use. On demand media is sent through Hypertext Transfer Protocol (HTTP) and can be housed on a regular Web server.

Library Uses

Libraries have found some innovative uses for streaming media. Many library Web sites link to sites with streaming media or purchase access to streaming educational videos, while others tackle the conversion of

conventional video and audio into Web-readable formats. Some libraries develop streaming media themselves, or find new ways to incorporate multimedia into library services.

Tulsa City-County Library in Oklahoma has recently begun linking
its catalog records to streaming video author interviews. When a user
clicks on a title to see the full record, he may see a link inviting him to
watch the interview. Users are given a choice of watching with Real or
Windows Media Player. This exciting project is just beginning and prom-
ises to add a new level of information to the library catalog.

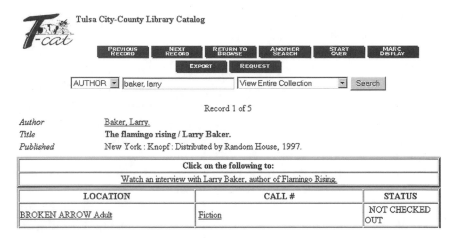

Figure 4-13. Tulsa City-County Library Catalog Record
www.tulsalibrary.org
An author search for Baker, Larry results in a list of titles. The full record for the
book *The Flamingo Rising* includes a link to watch a video of the author.

Figure 4-14. Author Interview in RealOne
The author video launches in the user-designated player (either Real or Windows Media).

Jimmy Ghaphery, a librarian at Cabell Library, Virginia Commonwealth University, has used RealSlideshow to produce a tutorial explaining how to find books at the library. Slides similar in look to those created by Microsoft's PowerPoint illustrate points made by the streaming audio narration. The automatic transition between slides is smooth; written captions provide an abbreviated commentary for users whose computers lack sound cards or have the computer volume turned down.

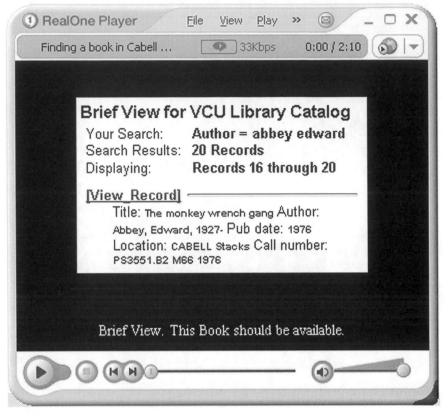

Figure 4-15. Cabell Library, Virginia Commonwealth University
www.library.vcu.edu/help/books.html

As mentioned before, other players on the market are threatening
Real's dominance. The library projects mentioned here provide further
proof of the competition; users are given the choice of using Real or others, like Windows Media Player and Flash.

While it makes sense to provide users a venue to watch and hear Real
files, librarians might be right to hesitate to install RealOne on public
computers. RealOne is huge, sluggish, and in the authors' experience,
the most instable of the multimedia players. Librarians might be wise
to wait to upgrade until Real has released an improved version of
RealOne. In the meantime, libraries can still download RealPlayer 8.0
from www.real.com. RealPlayer 8.0 has its annoying features, but it does
not appear to crash systems or bring up as many error messages as
RealOne.

WINDOWS MEDIA PLAYER

Purpose

In the past, Windows Media Player, or WMP, has lagged behind other players such as RealPlayer and even WinAMP. With the release of version 7.0, Microsoft vastly improved their player, bundling together more features and renovating the design of the player itself.

WMP 7 features a CD player, audio and video player, Internet radio, media jukebox and guide, and an application to create audio CDs with the appropriate drive. The player supports numerous file formats, including WAV, MIDI, AU, MPEG, MP3, and AVI. It can be used to play files found on the Web, but is not a part of the browser.

Users can transfer music files from the player to their personal PDAs, such as the PalmPilot or Handspring, using the Portable Device feature of the player. Users can also configure the look of the player by applying "skins." WMP comes with half a dozen skins, changing the player into a small toolbar, a clock with eyes in place of hours, or an alien head. Users can choose various visualizations to accompany audio files, providing them with a laser-light show that reacts to the beats of the music. Additional skins and visualizations can be downloaded from the Web. (Skins and visualizations are not available in the Mac versions.)

Users of 7.0 should consider upgrading to 7.1. The newest version looks identical to its predecessor, but improves the sound quality and closes some security holes in the player.

System Requirements

Processor:	266 MHz
Operating Systems:	Windows 98 and higher
Installed RAM:	64 MB
Browsers:	Netscape 4.X or greater, Internet Explorer 4.X or greater, can also run as helper application
File Size:	5.8 MB for Player, 21.4 MB including all components

Internet Explorer 5.5SP2 and 6.0 and Netscape 6.X Compatibility

As it is a fellow Microsoft product, Windows Media Player works well with Internet Explorer 5.5 and 6.0. Netscape users must be sure to have WMP 7.1; this version of the player should work well with Netscape 6.X.

Pros and Cons

Windows Media Player combines features that used to require numerous players: WinAMP for sound and visualizations; RealPlayer or

QuickTime for videos; RealJukebox for listening to Internet radio. Additionally, WMP can be used to create and export files. This variety of skills could easily have led to a confusing, crowded interface, but in fact, the interface is neatly laid out, with a standard menu along the top and large, functional buttons on the left-hand side.

WMP's behind-the-scenes strength is its high-level encoding. The player records audio better and downloads streaming files faster than Real. Its proprietary file type, WMA, has a higher quality sound and smaller file size than even MP3s. Its video output is equally impressive: clear, with sharp details and synchronized sound.

Unfortunately, this player cannot completely replace other video/audio players just yet. Although it plays MP3 files, it cannot record in that format. This may be a benefit to public libraries that are worried about the copyright aspects involved with MP3 creation by their patrons, but could be problematic for institutions trying to develop MP3s legally. Of more serious concern is the player's incompatibility with Real files: it cannot play them at all. Microsoft's strategy may be to wean people away from Real by denying access to its rival's files, but for the average user it is just inconvenient. Equally annoying, WMP 7x is not available for Windows 95 or NT. Once again, Microsoft is taking advantage of its player's popularity to encourage user behavior (in this case, upgrading Windows) that might not be feasible.

Most plug-ins and helper applications are created for individual rather than group use; WMP is no exception. Users can customize the player in any number of ways, including uploading personal play lists, burning CD tracks into portable files, transforming the player into different layouts, and changing options to increase the functionality of specific tasks. This makes the player an incredibly versatile tool, and could present a nightmare for librarians. Keeping WMP up and running on public machines with many different users can be time consuming. The Troubleshooting section touches on some of the most common problems encountered with WMP, but users should not hesitate to search the Web for answers to their particular troubles.

Examples

AUDIBLE.COM

www.audible.com

Figure 4-16. Audio Book on WMP

Audiobooks can be purchased through this Web site and listened to using Windows Media Player. As there is no video to play, WMP substitutes one of its visualizations, which ebbs and flows according to the narrator's voice. The book being read is identified beneath the screen as "Album." In this case, we are listening to *The Hobbit*.

Courtesy of Audible, Inc. Copyright © 2001

NASA

www.jsc.nasa.gov/er/seh/movies.html

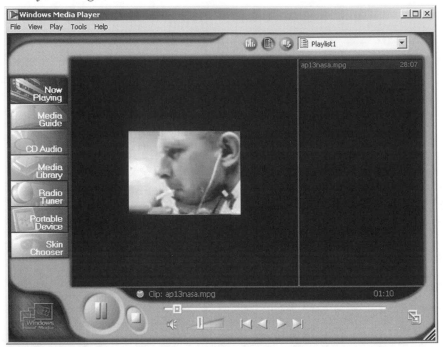

Figure 4-17. National Aeronautics and Space Administration
NASA provides movies in MOV (QuickTime), AVI, and streaming media format on its Web site. The above is a streaming media movie from NASA about the disaster-filled Apollo 13 mission.

SMITHSONIAN NATIONAL ZOO

pandas.si.edu/pandacam/videostream/pandavideocam1.htm

Figure 4-18. Smithsonian National Zoo
Smithsonian National Zoo provides two streaming video cameras for people to watch the Giant Pandas. In this example, the player is embedded within the browser so that a separate player is not launched. Only 60 concurrent users are allowed, so after ten minutes of observing the pandas play, users are sent to another page to watch real-time still images of the pandas.
Courtesy of the Smithsonian's National Zoological Park. One time permission.

Finding and Installing

Users should use the browser they intend to use most often to download the player and go to www.microsoft.com/windows/windowsmedia/en/download/default.asp. There is a link to this page from the opening screen of the Windows Media Player site, but it is well hidden.

The download page will prompt the user for his or her operating system and language preferences, then send the executable file to be downloaded. The file can be saved to the desktop and opened later, or run at that time. When the file is executed, the user will be walked through the installation process with wizard-type dialog boxes. Users should carefully read the privacy agreement as it includes directions to turn off some possibly intrusive components of WMP. Libraries concerned with patron confidentiality may wish to disengage the default setting, "Allow Internet sites to uniquely identify your player." These settings can be changed in the Options menu of the player.

During the installation, users can decide which files WMP should be used to read, and whether a quick launch icon for the player should be added to the desktop and programs toolbar. In some instances, the icons are added despite the user's chosen preferences. Right-clicking on the unwanted icon will pop up a menu list including a "delete" command. Choosing this menu option will remove the icon but not the program itself.

The player may have difficulty launching from a browser other than the one used to download it. For example, if Internet Explorer was used to get the player, Netscape may have trouble finding it. Downloading the player a second time in the other browsers, or manually registering it as a plug-in will solve the problem.

Troubleshooting

Problem: How can I tell if I need to upgrade my existing WMP?

Solution: While online, start the player. Under the "Help" menu, choose "Check for player upgrades..." The program will tell you if you have the latest version or which components you are missing. The Windows Media Component Setup wizard will walk you through the process of updating your player if needed.

Problem: I'm having difficulty with the video/sound.

Solution: The problem may lie in your sound or video drivers rather than in the player. If your drivers are updated, then check the hardware acceleration settings. For sound problems, this is located on the computer. From the Control Panel, choose Multimedia (or Sounds and Multimedia). Click on the Audio tab and under Sound Playback choose Advanced. This brings up the Advanced Audio Properties dialog box; choose the Performance tab. Drag the Hardware Acceleration scroll bar to None, and click OK. (If this does not work, you can repeat this procedure and click on the Restore Default Settings in the Performance box.) For video problems, adjust the hardware acceleration within Windows Media Player. From Tools menu, choose Options, then Performance. Once again, you have the ability to drag the scroll bar to None.

Problem: The video is playing very slowly and the sound is distorted.

Solution: WMP is playing the file as it downloads, so you are seeing it a portion at a time rather than at a constant rate. Even the fastest connections can have this problem. You can hit the "stop" button on the player; it will continue to download without playing it simultaneously. You can follow the progress of the download by watching the status bar to the right of the play/stop/pause controls. Once the file is completely downloaded, you can then watch the file without the starts and stops. Alternatively, you can save the file to the desktop or disk and then play it with WMP.

Problem: I'm having problems playing a CD (including headphone problems and computer lock ups).

Solution: WMP's default is for digital playback of CDs. This allows for high-quality sound but can cause the CD to skip, disable the headphone jack, or lock up the computer. From the Tools menu, choose Options, then CD Audio. Uncheck "Digital Playback," setting the playback to Analog. Warning: this will disable the visualizations feature.

Creating Files

Different programs can be used to create video and audio files. Users can download for free, or for 30-day trials, a number of tools that will convert CD music tracks to MP3s, AU, WAV, etc. Camcorders now provide digital video options, in which case the video can be directly uploaded to a computer, and various editing programs can finish the product. Video files cannot be created with WMP, but audio files are easily captured with the player.

From the Tools menu, choose Options, and click on CD audio tab. Check the Digital Copying box if it is not already marked, and set the quality of the recording with the slide bar. Remember, the smaller the file size the lower the quality of the sound. In the Archive section, check to see where the new file will be saved, and change accordingly. Click OK.

Put the CD in the computer, and in the player, click on the CD Audio button on the left-hand side. Check the boxes next to the tracks you want to copy. Then, click on the Copy Music button at the top of the screen. Be patient and do not switch to other programs while the music is being copied as this can lead to skips in your music.

Library Uses

The Hawaii Internet Public Library has found a use for the Microsoft Windows Media Player in its virtual library at netlibrary.net/eMusic/eMusicWorldHome.html. The library is beta testing a program in which a digital work can be lent to a patron for a designated length of time. Computer files of just about any type, particularly music and video, would be converted into lending library format (LLF). A patron receiving material in LLF could then use the file on his own computer until the borrowing period was over, at which time the file would expire. The lending library format sets a viewable time and makes it exceedingly difficult for the patron to save the file to his desktop. Read more about the LLF at www.archive.org/llf.html.

Lending library format files can currently be viewed by installing a filter for Windows Media Player 7.X. At the moment, only Windows machines can run this filter, but plans are being made to offer Mac and Linux versions. Much of this exciting project is a work in process. As of 2001, the Hawaii Internet Public Library's site offered time-limited access to a handful of artists' songs, but its long-term goal is to offer approximately 2500 albums in LLF.

WINAMP

Purpose

While Real, QuickTime, and Windows Media Player may be the big names in the player business, WinAMP has cultivated a steady and devoted audience. Created by Nullsoft, which was bought by giant AOL, WinAMP is an audio player that supports audio CDs, streaming audio files, and numerous sound file types, including WMA, WAV, and MP3.

When first downloaded, WinAMP includes the player, a play list, an equalizer to adjust sound quality, and a mini-browser to view certain videos. WinAMP's power can be greatly increased by downloading a myriad of free plug-ins, allowing the user to improve the sound quality, and arrange how WinAMP works. With hundreds of plug-ins available, the options are nearly overwhelming.

Users can change the look of the player with "skins" available from the WinAMP site. The generic player is bland looking, but the more than 20,000 skins give the player color, streamlined controls, and background images such as Britney Spears. Users who want to watch something while listening to music can download visualizations, color patterns that respond to the beats in music.

WinAMP's strength lies in its online community; the WinAMP site encourages people to create and share plug-ins and skins. The Nullsoft Developer section contains many pages of documentation detailing how to create new features for the player. Other sections are devoted to promoting these features. New users can look at plug-ins and skins based on type, popularity, or rating score. Each feature has a description and often a user review.

System Requirements

Processor: 486 Pentium; Power PC Macintosh
Operating Systems: Windows 95 and higher; Mac OS 8.5 and higher
                      (but not OS X)
Installed RAM: 48 MB
File Size: 1.1 MB for PCs; 174 KB for Macs

Internet Explorer 5.5SP2 and 6.0 and Netscape 6.X Compatibility

WinAMP users have reported some problems with IE 6.0; specifically, that the player skips when the user clicks on a link in the browser. Apparently, this happens in older computers because this version of IE and WinAMP share the same sound outlets; IE is trying to make a clicking sound while WinAMP is trying to play music, and both hiccup. This can be solved by upgrading the sound cards and drivers. As of yet, Netscape does not seem to be causing any problems.

Pros and Cons

WinAMP is the geek's choice of players. The plug-ins and skins make it the most customizable of all the multimedia players available. As the WinAMP site says, "We leave it up to you to make WinAMP exactly what you want it to be." Its reputation for small file size and stability are strong points as well. And while Real and Windows Media Player have been brawling and refusing to play one another's proprietary file formats, WinAMP has largely stayed above the fray, expending its energies towards playing as many formats as possible rather than trying to render other formats extinct. Plug-ins allow users to play both Real and Windows Media audio files.

Many WinAMP users are enthusiastic, loyal supporters of the player. These people are the ones constantly volunteering their time and energy developing new features to improve WinAMP. This grassroots approach makes WinAMP the most fun of the players. Its Web site's humorous tone is a good reflection of the player's image. Clicking on a link reading "What is WinAMP?", brings up a page declaring "What is WinAMP? A player you say? No, no baby. WinAMP is much more than that. WinAMP is a lifestyle. It is freestyle. Give me a word. Versatility? Yeah. Visionary? Of course. Community? Now you're talking."

Despite being owned by AOL, the player does not appear to be trying to make money. There are no advertisements in the player, no endless pitches to buy the "professional" version of WinAMP or software to create special WinAMP files. It is quite a relief to be free of the endless barrage of commercialism found in Real and WMP.

But WinAMP has its detractors. The original version of WinAMP that is first downloaded is not impressive-looking and in fact, a bit confusing. The mini-browser is tied to the audio files, but it looks like the user should be able to visit Web pages using the feature. The equalizer gives the user control over the audio output, but is probably more than the average library user might want to know. The plug-ins are wonderful extensions for WinAMP, but deciding which of the nearly 500 plug-ins should be downloaded is asking a bit much of the casual user. For the general public that simply wants to listen to some music, WinAMP may be overly complicated.

WinAMP currently has an alpha test version of its player for Macintosh, but it is not as complete as the PC version. The Mac version can play MP3s and the SHOUTcast broadcasts, but cannot make use of the plug-ins or skins.

Examples

WinAMP Player

www.winamp.com

Figure 4-19. Generic Version of WinAMP
The generic version of WinAMP is functional but not especially attractive. The WinAMP browser on the right is used to navigate to specific WinAMP sites and is not meant to replace the user's Web browser.

Secret Starfish Skin

www.winamp.com/skins

Figure 4-20. Seashell Skin
This skin uses a seashell motif. In general, the skins do not include a new look for the mini-browser.
Courtesy of Nini Katranouschkova

OCEAN SKIN

www.winamp.com/skins

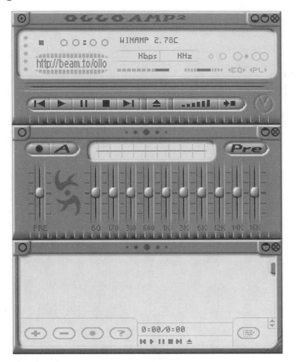

Figure 4-21. Ocean Skin
Many of the WinAMP skins are more streamlined and appeal to the technology-oriented people who support WinAMP.
Courtesy of Oliver Muller

Finding and Installing

WinAMP can be freely downloaded from the WinAMP site, www.winamp.com. The home page of the site has a bold link for downloading, and a graphical link encouraging users to "Get WinAMP NOW!"

The downloading page is designed for PC users but includes a link to the alpha version for Mac users. PC Windows users can choose from Lite, Standard, or Full versions. All three include MP3 and SHOUTcast support, as well as access to plug-ins and skins, but the Standard version supports visualizations while the Full version can play the Windows Media Audio format.

After choosing the appropriate version, the user clicks on the download link and saves the file to the computer. Double-clicking on the WinAMP setup icon will launch an installation wizard that will walk the user through the remainder of the process. WinAMP has help screens detailing the installation steps for Internet Explorer, Netscape, and AOL.

Installing new plug-ins and skins is very simple. Find the desired feature and click on the download link. The WinAMP site automatically saves the file into the correct location on the computer, and next time the player is opened, the skin or plug-in will be available. WinAMP is careful to warn that these features may not work right or may crash the computer; the user assumes any risk.

Troubleshooting

Problem: How do I change skins or visualizations?

Solution: In the top left-hand corner of the WinAMP player is a small icon, usually a button or squiggle shape, that serves as a menu marker. Clicking on it drops the menu; one of the choices is Options. Then choose Preferences. Visualizations is listed underneath Plug-Ins. A menu dialog box makes it easy to choose the feature you want.

Problem: I've tried downloading the skins, but it doesn't install automatically.

Solution: Try saving the file to your desktop; it can even be a zipped file. Have the file extract to the Skins folder, which by default is at C:\Program Files\WinAMP\Skins. Restart WinAMP; the skin should now be a choice in the menu.

Problem: I'm unhappy with the sound.

Solution: Try adjusting the slider controls in the equalizer panel of the player. If this does not help, the problem may be your computer's sound card. If you cannot fix the sound card, WinAMP has plug-ins, such as Waveout, which might help balance and volume control.

Problem: Where can I go for further help?

Solution: WinAMP's site www.winamp.com has extensive documentation, a detailed FAQ, and interactive forums to post questions. Most answers can be found by visiting this site.

Creating Files

WinAMP not only plays many audio files, it can be used to create the WAV type. This is of importance to anyone who wants to have files that will play in a regular CD player. MP3s may be smaller, but they cannot be heard on a stereo system; WAV files can. WinAMP is installed with a plug-in called Nullsoft Disk Writer. Changing the player from the regular output plug-in to the Disk Writer, then playing the items listed in the play list will result in these files becoming WAV files. The user decides where the files are stored. A CD burner is needed to transfer the WAVs to the actual compact disk.

Library Uses

As mentioned before, WinAMP's high-level of customization may make it difficult for the occasional user. However, numerous WinAMP fans may visit the library and expect to be able to access their favorite player on the public access machines. Since WinAMP fans tend to be technologically advanced, they may find a way to put it on the computers if it is not currently available.

With its smaller file size and reputation for stability, WinAMP may prove to be a good choice for libraries with older computers and limited RAM. Libraries planning to go this route should install the plug-ins giving the player support for Real and Windows Media formats. Additional plug-ins give WinAMP video playing abilities. With these features, a library could forego installing these larger multimedia players.

On the librarian's side of the desk, professionals might be interested in WinAMP's relationship with CDDB. CDDB is an Internet database of album information; it is compatible with many players, but is best known for its association with WinAMP. When a music CD is played in WinAMP, the player contacts CDDB and downloads the artist, title, and track information (including time lengths). This information is then displayed in WinAMP's play list. Without CDDB, the player cannot provide any information about the CD. Librarians have explored using CDDB as a cataloging tool, particularly for MARC records. Nothing has been done officially yet, but it is an interesting premise. For further information about CDDB, visit www.gracenote.com.

Chapter 5

Math and Science Tools

OVERVIEW

Plug-ins for math and science help represent difficult concepts, illustrate models of science not visible with the naked eye, and allow users to modify equations and to problem-solve. Usually, they are designed for a higher-level audience: researchers, professionals in the field, or advanced students.

The programs in this chapter are highly specialized tools not intended for general audiences. Libraries that support patrons in math and science, such as academic libraries, will find these tools useful in public computing areas. Other libraries will decide that the tools are not appropriate for their audiences. However, libraries that maintain lists of Web resources in mathematics and the sciences, either on their Web sites or in their online catalogs, may want to provide a link to the appropriate site where patrons can download these tools.

CHIME/RASMOL/CN3D

Purpose

Chime, RasMol, and Cn3D are programs that display 1D, 2D, and 3D molecular structures. The 3D structures can be manipulated (rotated, translated, zoomed) and displayed in different chemical model formats such as "ball and stick" or "wireframe." Users can view proteins, chemicals, drugs, crystals, and other molecular biology and biochemistry models from the inside out including the elements that comprise the structure, the bonds that hold the structure together, and the structure's rotation. Cn3D displays 1D and 3D versions of the structure that are linked together so that clicking in the 1D version highlights the corresponding area in the 3D version.

RasMol, named for **Ras**ter **Mol**ecules, was developed by a British computer science student named Roger Sayle. When he received his PhD in 1993, he made his program freely available to the scientific community. In 1999, Sayle stopped revision of his software and newer versions have been produced by Herbert Bernstein. The program is still freely available and its code is open source and has been adapted through the years by various sources. The most well-known derivative of RasMol is the MDL Chime program. Chime, **Ch**emical **Mime**, was released in 1996. Chime, like RasMol, is free. However, where RasMol is freely distributed, Chime is only available from MDL. Cn3D ("See in 3-D") was developed by the National Center for Biotechnology Information (NCBI) for use with the Entrez database, which includes protein and polynucleotide structures.

RasMol is a helper application; Chime runs inside the browser window. Both programs have the same functionality and similar menu options. The most common file types for molecular structure are MDL Molfile (MOL) and Brookhaven Protein Databank (PDB) files. Cn3D is a helper application that displays PDB files that have been validated and corrected. Although the program will not display basic PDB files, users can save basic PDB files with the viewer and then display them in Chime or RasMol.

System Requirements

CHIME:

Processor: Pentium processor or Power PC
Operating Systems: Windows 95 or higher, Mac OS 8.6 or higher
Installed RAM: 64MB for PC, 32MB for Macintosh
Browsers: PC and Mac: Netscape 4.7X; PC only: Internet Explorer 4.0-5.5SP2
                             Note: Chime will not run with Internet Explorer on a Mac. Netscape is required.
Monitor Resolution: 800 × 600 recommended

RASMOL:

Processor: Minimum requirements not defined
Operating Systems: Windows 3.1 or higher, Mac System 7.0 or higher
Installed RAM: 64MB for PC, 32MB for Macintosh
Browsers: Netscape 3.X or higher, Internet Explorer 3.X or higher

Cn3D:

Processor:	Pentium processor or Power PC
Operating Systems:	Windows 95 or higher, Mac OS 8.6 or higher
Browsers:	Netscape 4.X or higher, Internet Explorer 4.X or higher
Color (Cn3D):	16-bit high color display is recommended for Windows machines, ATI Rage graphics cards are recommended for Macintosh machines

Internet Explorer 5.5 SP2 and 6.0 and Netscape 6.X Compatibility

Chime is incompatible with both Netscape 6.0 and Internet Explorer 6.0, but Chime 2.6 SP3 will work with Internet Explorer 5.5 SP2. MDL is working on a fully compatible version. RasMol as a helper application will work for files saved from within any version of Internet Explorer or Netscape. Cn3D is also fully compatible.

Pros and Cons

Molecular visualization software is designed for a specific audience. If a library supports patrons in the fields of molecular biology, biochemistry, medicine, chemistry, or pharmacy, these tools are an important addition to the desktop. However, libraries that serve the general population will probably not need to install these tools.

Molecular model files tend to be large and require fast computers with large amounts of memory to work well in a viewer. Only the most robust machines should be used to support the software.

If a library would like to support molecular model visualization, but would rather not support three new software tools, one of the three tools will suffice. Libraries that support Netscape (but not version 6) should install Chime because it is the most integrated of the three programs. It runs inside the browser window and supports all of the file types the patrons are likely to encounter. Libraries that support Internet Explorer or Netscape 6 or a combination of browsers should consider RasMol. Although as a helper application it is not as seamless as Chime, the program will support all file types and work with all of the browser versions. Files from the Entrez database can be viewed with Chime or RasMol, but will lose some of the Cn3D viewing features. Cn3D is most likely to be installed only in special libraries that support basic scientists who rely on the Entrez system.

Examples

DIAMOND PDB FILE IN CHIME

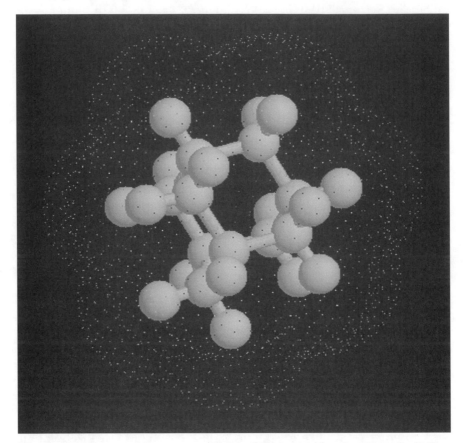

Figure 5-1. Diamond Structure in Ball and Stick with Van der Waals Radii Dot Surface Format
We thank Paul M. Lahti, Chemistry Department, University of Massachusetts at Amherst, for the use of these materials.

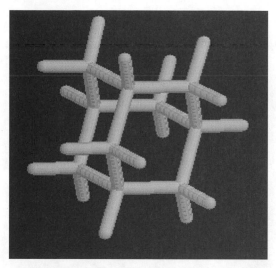

Figure 5-2. Diamond Structure in Sticks Format

With this file, users can view the inside of a diamond in a variety of formats including Wireframe, Ball and Stick, Sticks, and Spacefill. An example of the diamond crystal on the Web can be found at Nova: The Diamond Deception www.pbs.org/wgbh/nova/diamond/inside.html where it is available in both a small segment for detail and a large segment for overall structure.

We thank Paul M. Lahti, Chemistry Department, University of Massachusetts at Amherst, for the use of these materials.

SMELLS DATABASE

mc2.cchem.berkeley.edu/Smells

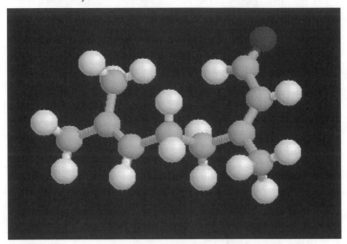

Figure 5-3. ChemConnections Web Site at UC Berkeley

The ChemConnections Web site at UC Berkeley provides 3D images of chemicals that smell, listed by their chemical and common name. Some of the odors listed are 2-Phenylethanol (roses), Allicin (garlic), Eucalyptol (menthol), and Eugenol (cloves). The image pictured above is 3,7-Dimethyl-2, 6-octadienal, common name Geranial/Citral A, which smells like lemons and is displayed in ball and stick format.

This material is based upon work supported by the National Science Foundation grant No. DUE-9455924, Copyright ©1998 by the Regents of the University of California

UNIVERSITY OF MASSACHUSETTS DNA VIEWER

www.umass.edu/microbio/chime/dna

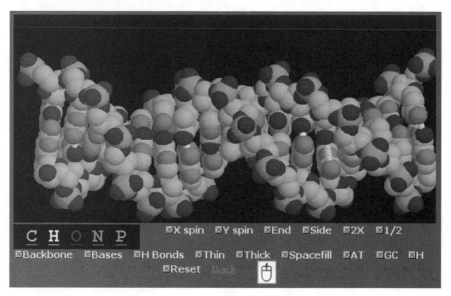

Figure 5-4. University of Massachusetts DNA Molecule
In addition to the standard function of RasMol and Chime, the UMass DNA molecule can be manipulated to show AT and GC bonds and the DNA Backbone.

Finding and Installing

RasMol: RasMol can be downloaded from a number of different sites. Both version 2.6 and 2.7 and their supporting documentation and the original source code can be downloaded at www.umass.edu/microbio/rasmol/getras.htm. When installing RasMol on Windows 95 machines, the installer will not create an icon on the desktop or in the Start Menu. To add an icon to either place, locate the downloaded file and drag it to the desktop or to the menu.

Chime: Chime can be downloaded at the MDL Web site at www.mdlchime.com/chime. Registration is required. During the installation process, Chime will locate the browsers installed on the local machine and configure the plug-in to launch all PDB and MOL files.

If both Chime and RasMol are installed on the same computer, clicking on a file on a Web page will open the file in Chime. To view the file in RasMol, simply save the file in Chime, open RasMol, and open the file that was just saved.

Cn3D: Cn3D can be downloaded at www.ncbi.nlm.nih.gov/Structure/

CN3D/cn3dinstall.shtml. After selecting the desired format, users will be prompted to download the self-install program to their hard drive. The first time an Entrez structure file is selected in the Web browser, users will be prompted to select the Cn3D viewer as the desired viewer.

Troubleshooting

Problem: When I print with RasMol, the resolution is poor. How can I print a higher quality image?

Solution: RasMol has the capabilities of converting your file into a GIF image. While viewing your structure, select the Export menu and choose GIF. Open the GIF file in a graphic manipulation program, such as Photoshop or PaintShop Pro, and print the file from that program.

Problem: I want to print my Cn3D structure. Where is the print function?

Solution: It is not possible to print from within the Cn3D program. If you wish to print a file, you should capture the window with the screenshot feature on your computer or with a graphics capture program. The image can then be copied into a word processor file or opened in an image manipulation program and printed using the print function of that program.

Problem: I want to zoom in on my structure. There is no zoom option on my RasMol menu, or in the Chime right mouse click pop-up box. How can I zoom?

Solution: You are right, there are options that are not listed in the menus that can be activated with mouse and keyboard commands. For a complete list, see the table below.

Action	Windows	Macintosh
Menu	Right	Hold Down
Rotate X,Y	Click/Drag	Click/Drag
Translate X,Y	Ctrl-Right/Drag	Command/Drag
Rotate Z	Shift-Right/Drag	Shift-Command/Drag
Zoom	Shift-Left	Shift

Mouse Click Summary

Creating Files

Structure files are created using RasMol Script. In addition, there are added Chime commands. To view a list of RasMol and Chime scripts go to www.mdlchime.com/chime/dev/rasmol.asp. You may have to register with Chime and login to view the page.

The RasMol program includes a command line component that can be used to create structures.

MDL, the makers of Chime, also distribute a program for developing 2D and 3D structures called ISIS/Draw. For more information about ISIS/Draw, visit www.mdli.com/downloads/isis.draw/isisdrawreg.html.

Cn3D files are only available from the MMDB database from the National Center for Biotechnology Information. The MMDB database is a subset of files from the Brookhaven Protein Databank that have been translated into the ASN.1 format.

Library Uses

RasMol, Chime, and Cn3D are most relevant to academic libraries that support computer science, biology, chemistry, medical school basic sciences, or pharmacy programs. Libraries that maintain categorized Web lists in any of these subjects should provide links to sites that provide molecular visualization files and sites to download the programs.

The National Center for Biotechnology Information, part of the National Library of Medicine, provides the MMDB database as part of Entrez. When searching any of the NCBI databases, such as PubMed or Entrez Protein, citations that contain a protein structure will provide a link for viewing the file in Cn3D or RasMol.

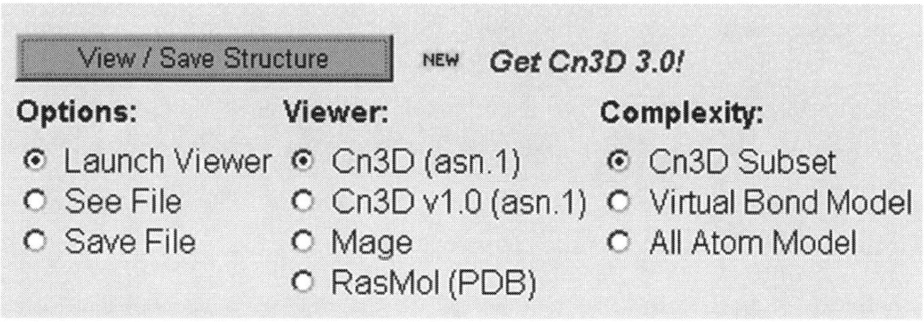

Figure 5-5. View a Structure in Cn3D
Selecting the option to Launch Viewer in the Cn3D (asn.1) Viewer will launch the Cn3D file and display the file.

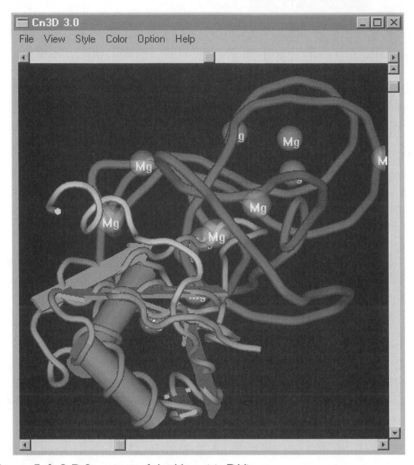

Figure 5-6. 3-D Structure of the Hepatitis D Virus

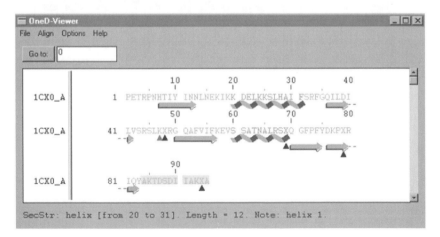

Figure 5-7. Protein Structure of the Hepatitis D Virus

This structure is a portion of the Hepatitis D virus as displayed in Cn3D. The top window displays the 3D structure of the file while the bottom window displays the protein sequence of the structure. The area highlighted in yellow on the 1D page, highlights the corresponding portion of the structure in the 3D view.

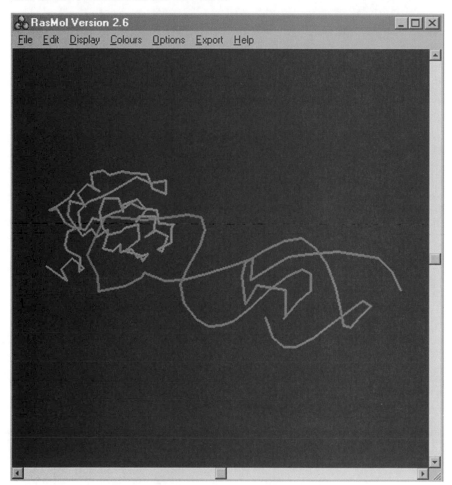

Figure 5-8. Basic PBD File of the Hepatitis D Virus
The same structure opened as a basic PDB file in RasMol.

LIVEMATH

Purpose

LiveMath Maker is a tool that is used to make mathematics on the Web more interactive and fun. Users of LiveMath Maker can create fully contained math problems and solutions called notebooks. Notebooks can be placed on the Web so that visitors to a Web site can interact with the equations. The LiveMath plug-in is required to view the notebooks.

LiveMath began in the early 1990s as Expressionist, and has undergone many name changes over the years. The current program, LiveMath, is owned and distributed by Theorist Interactive, LLC. The creator of the software, Allan Bonadio, wanted to make math come to life and provide an environment where students can explore math in a highly interactive way.

To make the files more interactive, LiveMath has the ability to create notebooks that accept input from the user. Students can change values in an equation or calculate the unknowns and input the answer into the formulas, change the plotting of a graph, and manipulate images to illustrate problems. The LiveMath plug-in shows notebooks created for all levels of math including pre-algebra, algebra, geometry, trigonometry, and calculus (including 3D files).

System Requirements

Processor:	486 PC or greater; 68K Mac or greater
Operating Systems:	Windows 95 or greater; Macintosh System 7.5.3-OS9
Installed RAM:	32MB minimum
Browsers:	Netscape 3.X or greater, Internet Explorer 4.X or greater
File Size:	2MB

Internet Explorer 5.5 SP2 and 6.0 and Netscape 6.X Compatibility

LiveMath is fully compatible with all recent versions of both browsers.

Pros and Cons

The interactivity that LiveMath provides makes working with the notebooks interesting. The graphs are clear and colorful and the animation helps to illustrate difficult problems. The plug-in also allows users to zoom in on an area of interest, and to move and rotate the file, or set the file in motion so that it rotates itself. Users can also adjust the accuracy of the plot. Higher accuracy files are smoother, but also take longer to redraw when moved.

LiveMath files contain visual cues that indicate where you can enter information to change the file. However, the graphics used are not intuitive. For example, LiveMath uses dialog bubbles, assumptions boxes, conclusion triangles, a knife, and a rocket, among other images. Also, because users can change any of the information in the equation, it is important to know what should be changed to achieve the appropriate outcome. Users should be encouraged to read the help files. LiveMath makes it easy by adding a Help link to the top of each notebook.

Examples

LINEAR EQUATION SOLUTION CHECKER

faculty.whatcom.ctc.edu/wwebber/lmstuff/algelm.htm

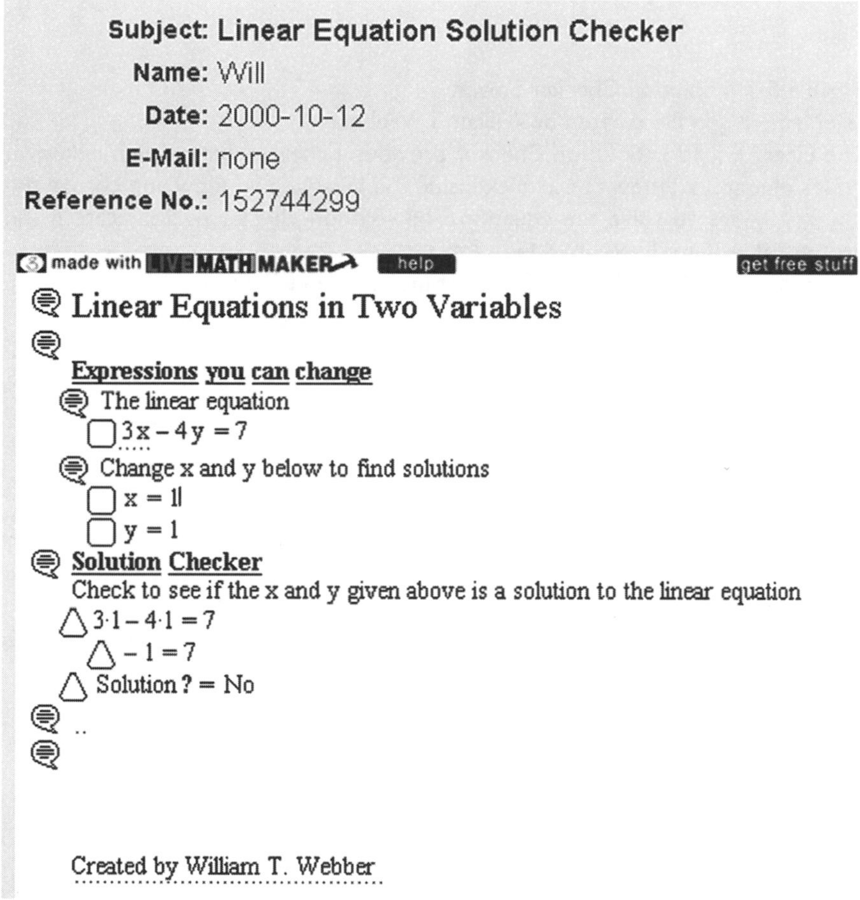

> **Subject: Linear Equation Solution Checker**
> **Name:** Will
> **Date:** 2000-10-12
> **E-Mail:** none
> **Reference No.:** 152744299
>
> ---
>
> [S] made with **LIVE MATH MAKER** [help] [get free stuff]
>
> ✇ **Linear Equations in Two Variables**
> ✇
>   **Expressions you can change**
>   ✇ The linear equation
>   ☐ $3x - 4y = 7$
>   ✇ Change x and y below to find solutions
>   ☐ $x = 1|$
>   ☐ $y = 1$
> ✇ **Solution Checker**
>   Check to see if the x and y given above is a solution to the linear equation
>   △ $3 \cdot 1 - 4 \cdot 1 = 7$
>   △ $-1 = 7$
>   △ Solution ? = No
> ✇ ..
> ✇
>
> Created by William T. Webber

Figure 5-9. Linear Equation Solution Checker
LiveMath Plug-in file created by William T. Webber
Created in LiveMath Maker for Theorist Interactive LLC

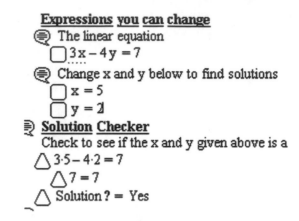

Figure 5-10. Solution Checker Solved
LiveMath Plug-in file created by William T. Webber
The Linear Equation Solution Checker provides a linear equation with unknown
values of x and y. Students can click inside the LiveMath window and change the
x and y values to solve the equation. The solution checker will indicate if the
proper values have been provided.
Created in LiveMath Maker for Theorist Interactive LLC

FRACTAL

www.eng.usf.edu/~tdavis/livemath/fractal.htm

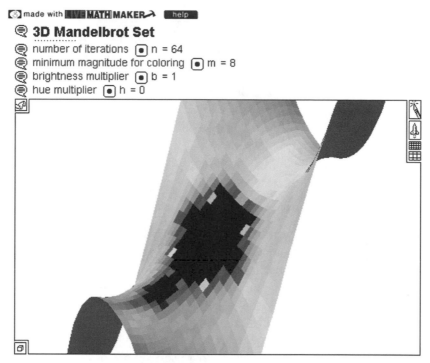

Figure 5-11. Mandelbrot Set Fractal

In addition to being able to rotate and zoom in on the fractal, each of the numbers at the top of the image can be changed to alter the fractal. Changes are reflected in the fractal image window.

Courtesy of Thomas G. Davis, Department of Civil and Environmental Engineering, University of South Florida, Tampa, FL 33620

Finding and Installing

LiveMath can be downloaded from the Theorist Interactive Web site at www.livemath.com. Choose the icon to download the LiveMath Plug-in. Users will be prompted to download a version that is most appropriate for their individual computing environment. Download options include a Java-based installer, and a minimum and full installer. For the plug-in, the minimum and full installers are equivalent. After running the installation, restarting the Web browser will complete the installation.

Troubleshooting

Problem: I used to have a program called MathPlus to view math files over the Internet. I've just switched to LiveMath and the software will not work. What's wrong?

Solution: Earlier versions of LiveMath were called MathPlus, Expressionist, Theorist, and MathView. These other programs may interfere with LiveMath. Uninstall all previous versions of the software, and then reinstall LiveMath to solve the problem.

Problem: I'm trying to use the Net-based installer, but my browser keeps hanging. How can I install the LiveMath Plug-in?

Solution: Net-based installers sometimes cause problems (for example, if you are behind a firewall). If you select the Minimum or Full Installer, you should have no trouble downloading and installing the file.

Creating Files

LiveMath files are created with LiveMath Maker. The creation program, also available at www.livemath.com, can be downloaded for a free 30-day trial. Notebooks are created using menus and an input palette that allows users to select the desired function and features. Parts of equations can be highlighted and dragged around within an equation; for example they can be relocated to the other side of the equal sign.

LiveMath comes with the Starter Library that provides hundreds of notebooks that can be customized so that users do not have to start each notebook from scratch. The starter files help even the newest user create useable files quickly and easily. More advanced users can choose to create their notebooks from scratch.

LiveMath notebooks can be embedded into Web pages to make files that can be uploaded to a Web server. Users may also take advantage of LiveMathBoard, an area on LiveMath's Web site where users can set up an account and post their LiveMath notebooks.

Library Uses

Although libraries are unlikely to produce LiveMath files, they may link to sites that require the LiveMath plug-in. Academic libraries that support mathematics programs are the best candidates for supporting LiveMath. Public and school libraries may consider supporting LiveMath so that students and teachers can explore sites specifically designed to help with homework. For example, the LiveMath site provides an answer checker for roots, logarithms, factors, and more. Students can enter their formulas and their answer and the plug-in will indicate if the answer is correct or incorrect. Online LiveMath graphing calculators can help illustrate graphs that are in color, animated, rotatable, and printable.

Chapter 6

Accessibility Tools

OVERVIEW

In 1998, the United States Congress amended the 1973 Rehabilitation Act, adding a requirement for federal agencies to make their electronic technology and information accessible to the disabled. Web sites were included in this law, known as Section 508. As Webmasters began to change designs to reflect the new rules, they realized much of the Web is far from compliant with Section 508. As technology advanced to include audio, video, and other file formats online, few people worried about who would be left behind by these developments.

At the same time, the Internet has grown to pervade all sections of the population. Not only the disabled have been inconvenienced by accessibility issues. Many senior citizens have become active Web users, but they can become frustrated at the small print of PDFs and image maps, or the mediocre sound quality of audio narration.

Web developers know accessibility is an issue when designing Web sites, but only the federal government sites must adhere to Section 508. The private sector is under no legal pressure to comply. Libraries involved with Web projects that may cause accessibility problems should investigate ways to ameliorate the situation. Multimedia creators may want to use MAGpie, a program developed by CPB/WGBH National Center for Accessible Media. This freely distributed software can be used to create captions for videos played in QuickTime, Windows Media Player, and Real. Those interested can read about and download MAGpie at www.webaim.org/howto/magpie/index.

This section concentrates on plug-ins that would be most useful for those on the other side of the computer: the person browsing the Web. The three tools explored here concentrate on helping those with visual impairments. The Web is such a visual medium; after all, what is the Web without graphics? It is Gopher, a system made virtually extinct by the invention of Web browsers that could display pictures. Adobe Access, Lens Magnifying Glass, and ReadMePlease can be used to show that even without the pretty pictures, the Web is darn useful!

ADOBE ACCESS

Purpose

One of the ongoing problems with Portable Document Format (PDF) files has been their inaccessibility by visually impaired users. Because PDF files, especially the older ones, are actually images of text rather than text itself, screen readers are useless; there is nothing for them to read.

As PDFs have become more popular, these concerns have increased. Even more important has been the federal government's decision to require any technology bought by government agencies be accessible by the disabled. Since the enacting of this law, there has been a mad scramble to make Web sites compliant. As the leading provider of software to create PDF files, Adobe has invested time and money into creating ways to make PDFs more usable.

For users with Adobe Acrobat Reader 4.0.5, Adobe created a plug-in called Adobe Acrobat Access. This tool provides a text version of PDF files. For creators of PDF files, Adobe offers the Make Accessible and Paper Capture Plug-Ins. The first plug-in can transform original PDFs into newer PDF versions with tags readable by screen readers. The Paper Capture Plug-In supplies optical character recognition to scanned documents. Finally, not a plug-in but worth mentioning is Adobe's Online Conversion Tools. Users can visit the Adobe site and type the full URL of the PDF file into an online form. Adobe will then generate a text version on the fly. A more advanced version of the form allows the user to decide which pages should be converted, and to provide a password if the PDF requires one. Users can also send an e-mail request for this service.

System Requirements

Processor: Intel 486
Operating Systems: Windows 95 through 2000
Installed RAM: 4 MB
Browsers: Should work with any browser
File Size: 1.3 MB
Other: Adobe Acrobat Reader 4.0 must be installed

Internet Explorer 5.5 SP2 and 6.0 and Netscape 6.X Compatibility

The Adobe Access Plug-In works best when the Reader launches as a helper application outside of the browser. It should cooperate with either of the newest browsers. Users may have to go to the Reader's Preferences and uncheck the Display PDF in Browser option.

Adobe Acrobat Reader 5.0 works best with the latest versions of Internet Explorer.

Pros and Cons

The Access plug-in was Adobe's first attempt at making PDF easier for disabled populations. Since the problem lay in screen readers' inabilities to read the PDFs, it seemed the obvious solution was to convert the files to readable text. This created a new set of problems, however. One of PDF's selling points has been its security; users could look at and print out a document but would not be able to change the wording. Once the document was turned into text, users could make any number of modifications.

In response, Adobe has encouraged users to move to Acrobat 5.0 and creators to use the Make Accessible Plug-In. Files in this system are a new type of PDF, ones that contain invisible tags readable by the screen readers. This preserves the integrity of the document itself. Unfortunately, this new solution has not worked as well as hoped. The text created by the older Access plug-in has had more success with the screen readers than the "accessible-tagged" PDFs. Additionally, creators of PDFs may choose to forego making their files accessible in order to ensure security.

With any of these tools, however, there is the need for proofreading. The text conversions have a high rate of successful character recognition, but unusual layouts and strange words cause mistakes. Any graphics, including pictures, charts, and tables, will most likely be discarded completely. PDF files with columns can be problematic.

The Adobe plug-ins work on Windows platforms but not Macintosh computers. Mac users can use the Online Conversion Tools to get a down-and-dirty text version of PDF files.

Examples

MINIMAL ELEMENTS FOR SCREENING, DIAGNOSIS, AND TREATMENT

mdpublichealth.org/cancer/html/colcan.html

Original PDF:

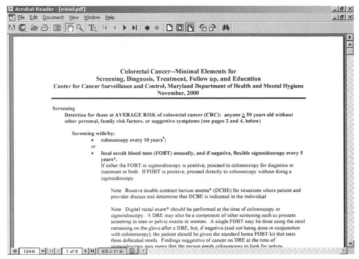

Figure 6-1. PDF Handout
Courtesy of MDPublicHealth.org (Maryland Department of Health and Mental
Hygiene, Family Health Administration)

After Adobe Access Plug-In:

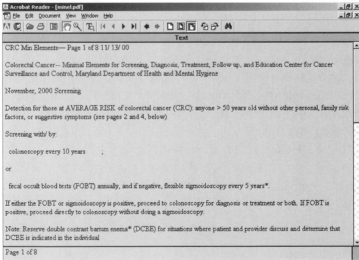

Figure 6-2. Text Version
This patient education site from Maryland placed handouts about colorectal cancer
on its Web site. While the textual version has lost the formatting, it is still readable.

10-YEAR SLE/INDIAN RIVER LAGOON TRIBUTARY BASIN AVERAGE ANNUAL FLOWS

www.sfwmd.gov/org/wrp/wrp_ce/2_wrp_ce_info/2_wrp_ce_maps.html

Original PDF:

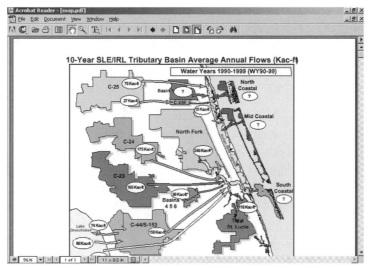

Figure 6-3. PDF Map
Map created by South Florida Water Management District

After Access Plug-In Conversion:

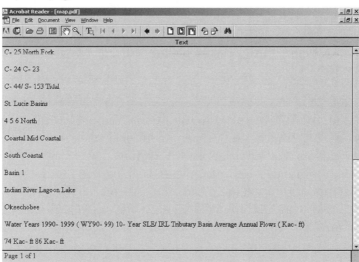

Figure 6-4. Text Version
This Florida government site put its maps in PDF for online viewing. As the map is a picture, the text translation does not make much sense.

Finding and Installing

All of the plug-ins for accessing or creating accessible PDF files can be found on the Adobe site at access.adobe.com. Users may download any of the tools, but installation can only occur if they have the correct program: Access requires Acrobat Reader 4.0; Make Accessible and Paper Capture require Adobe Acrobat 5.0. Readers can be downloaded for free, but the full-fledged Acrobat program to create PDF files costs $249.

Installation wizards walk the user through the rest of the process.

Troubleshooting

Problem: How do I see the text version of a PDF using Acrobat Reader 4?

Solution: Open the file outside the browser. See the chapter on Adobe Acrobat for a detailed description of this. Then, hold down the Control and 4 keys simultaneously. The PDF then turns into text. To return to the PDF view, hold down the Control and E keys together.

Problem: My computer came with Acrobat Reader 5; how can I find version 4?

Solution: Unfortunately, Adobe has taken down its link to download the earlier version of the Reader. Tucows, a wonderful resource for freeware and shareware, offers a free download of Acrobat Reader 4.0.5 under Windows 95/98, Imaging Tools. Tucows can be found at www.tucows.com.

Problem: I am using Internet Explorer 5.0 and am having difficulties with the accessibility portion of Adobe Acrobat Reader 5.0

Solution: Upgrading to Internet Explorer 5.5 should solve this problem. In fact, many aspects of Acrobat 5.0 will work better with the updated version of IE.

Creating Files

Adobe is urging PDF creators to use Adobe Acrobat 5.0 with the Make Accessible Plug-In. The full version of Acrobat places special tags into PDF documents that are readable by screen readers. Not everything can be accessible—images and complicated tables, for example—but the great majority of the document can be improved.

For people who wish to make scanned documents, there is the Paper Capture Plug-In. When a text document is scanned, the computer may store the scan as an image. The individual words are understood to be part of the image and do not have a separate identity. Paper Capture has OCR, which looks at each section of the image and tries to identify each letter, and how the letters are constructed into words. This process can be immensely easier than re-typing the document, but proof-reading must be done.

The Adobe accessibility tools are works in progress. Those who consider accessibility of files to be a priority should offer HTML or ASCII versions of the PDFs.

Library Uses

As mentioned in the chapter discussing Adobe Acrobat Reader, libraries may find many uses for PDF documents. Additionally, many popular Web sites offer information in this format. Libraries, particularly those with older populations, need to investigate ways to make PDF reading easier. Even people without visual problems have difficulties reading PDF files online; the files print beautifully but often look blurry on the screen.

Ideally, libraries could have Adobe Acrobat Readers versions 4 and 5 on their public access computers. This would allow users to choose whether to turn the files into text, or try and have the screen reader interpret the tagged PDF. If one did not work, users could try the other method. Unfortunately, Readers 4.X and 5.X do not share a computer well. At this point, Acrobat Reader 4 and its Access plug-in seem to have a better record. Libraries may want to stay with this older combination until Adobe works out the kinks in Reader 5.

LENS MAGNIFYING GLASS

Purpose

Lens Magnifying Glass was originally designed as a demonstration for ABF Software's krpRegions library, a group creating innovative interfaces. Lens quickly became more than a demo; it is a very useful tool for those with poor eyesight.

Lens is shaped like a large magnifying glass. On the handle of the glass are plus and minus signs; clicking on them zooms in or out of the item located within the glass itself. As the user moves the glass across the screen, whatever he passes over is magnified. Magnification can be one time to sixty-four times the normal view. The tool cannot be used to shrink the normal view.

When Lens is open, it will automatically lay itself over the active window. When a user changes windows, it is necessary to refresh Lens; until it is refreshed, Lens continues to magnify the last window visited. Hitting the Space key is an easy way to refresh Lens and have it ready to use in the new program.

Lens can be used in any program, but this chapter will concentrate on its Web applications.

System Requirements

Operating Systems: Windows 95 through 2000
File Size: 670 KB

Internet Explorer 5.5 SP2 and 6.0 and Netscape 6.X Compatibility

Lens is compatible with these browsers.

Pros and Cons

Lens is extremely simple to use. The magnified view appears within the magnifying glass, just like its real-life counterpart. The pluses and minuses allow for an unusual amount of control over how much the view should be magnified.

Right clicking on Lens will bring up a menu detailing keyboard shortcuts for refreshing the Lens, or magnifying to the limit. A Help section also provides some useful tips.

One rather large drawback to using Lens in a browser is that text that is magnified cannot be accessed by the mouse. Any hyperlinks that are magnified cannot be clicked on until the tool is away from that section of the screen. Additionally, Lens can only explore the parts of the screen that are visible on the monitor. Dragging Lens to the edge of the screen does not activate the scrolling. If the Web page is too long to fit onto the screen, the user must scroll to the new spot in the page and then refresh Lens.

Examples

CENSUS BUREAU MINORITY LINKS FOR MEDIA

www.census.gov/pubinfo/www/afamhot1.html

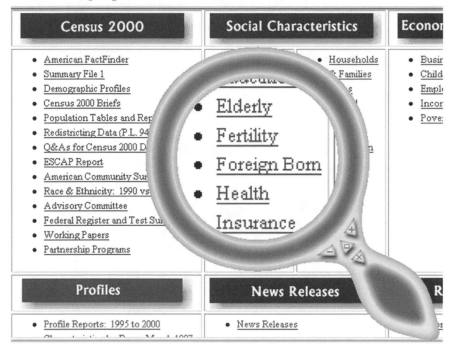

Figure 6-5. Census 2000 Lists
Long lists of resources can be magnified for easier viewing.

CENSUS 2000 BRIEFS AND SPECIAL REPORTS SERIES

www.census.gov/population/www/cen2000/briefs.html

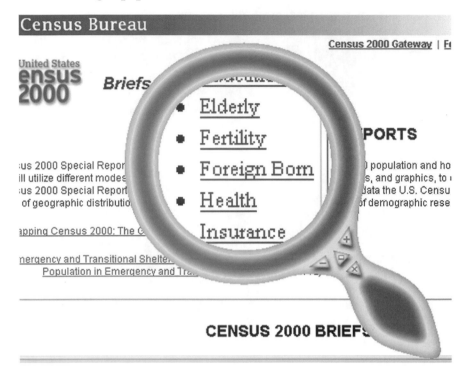

Figure 6-6. Magnification View Unchanged
If the user does not refresh Lens after changing pages or otherwise changing
the screen, the previous page visited will continue to be magnified.

Finding and Installing

Lens can be downloaded for free at ABF Software, www.abfsoftware.
com. An installation wizard will walk the user through the process.

Troubleshooting

Problem: I find it difficult to drag Lens around with my mouse.

Solution: Lens can be moved using the Right, Left, Up, and Down
arrow keys for greater precision. Holding down the Control or Shift keys
while dragging the Lens can also affect the speed.

Problem: Lens is not magnifying my active window.

Solution: You must refresh Lens whenever you change windows or
scroll within the current window. Click on Lens (a safe place is the rim
around the "glass"), then hit the Space bar.

Problem: I don't like how Lens looks.

Solution: ABF Software has developed some "skins" which can change the look of the tool. These files are available from the ABF Software site.

Library Uses

Many libraries have a magnifying glass tucked away in a drawer for use by patrons who need to look at a small-printed index or newspaper. Lens is an online equivalent of this. Anyone who has a visual impairment, or who has difficulty reading tiny text in an image map can appreciate Lens.

READPLEASE

Purpose

Money Tree Software first released ReadPlease in 2000; the newest version has a more intuitive interface and concentrates on its main purpose: translating text to speech. ReadPlease is a helper application that can be opened alongside the browser. Users copy ASCII text from a Web page and paste it into ReadPlease 2002's window. Hitting the play button then activates the voice, supplied by Microsoft Voice Engine, which reads aloud the text. Each word is highlighted as it is read.

ReadPlease comes in two varieties: free and Plus. The free version can be downloaded, or ordered on CD-ROM (which costs $12.99). The Plus version costs $49.99. Either version will read the text aloud, but the Plus version does have some nice features, such as making hyperlinks clickable within the ReadPlease window, and the ability to have the voice start reading at various points in the window. In the free version, the voice begins at the top of the document and works its way down. A pause button can provide breaks.

System Requirements

Processor:	Pentium 200
Operating Systems:	Windows 95 through XP
Installed RAM:	16 MB
Browsers:	Any browser that allows copying of text
Hard Disk Space:	20 MB
File Size:	9 MB

Internet Explorer 5.5 SP2 and 6.0 and Netscape 6.X Compatibility

Since ReadPlease works outside of the browser, it has no compatibility issues with the newer browsers.

Pros and Cons

ReadPlease 2002's interface is much improved from the 2000 version. ReadPlease 2000 had confusing dials and buttons, and text was displayed against an olive green background that did not provide much contrast. It looked very much like an onscreen version of a PDA. Unfortunately, most users who needed a screen reader like ReadPlease were not familiar with the layout of a PDA. This misstep in design led to ReadPlease 2000's induction into the Interface Hall of Shame, www.iarchitect.com/readplease.htm.

The new interface has buttons that look like the play, pause, and stop buttons on a VCR and the big multimedia players. The black text is displayed against a pale yellow background. The pulldown menus are at the default size, though, and may be difficult for visually impaired users.

ReadPlease works wonderfully as long as the text can be copied and pasted into its window. Text that is part of an image, such as in an image map or PDF document, cannot be used with ReadPlease. Libraries that plan to use this program with Web browsers should consider purchasing the Plus version. In the free version, hyperlinks within text cannot be clicked on. In the Plus version, they retain their clickability; once clicked upon, the new Web page will launch in the browser.

Money Tree currently has no plans to develop non-Windows versions of ReadPlease. Mac or UNIX users will have to look elsewhere for a reader.

Examples

READPLEASE **2002**

www.readplease.com

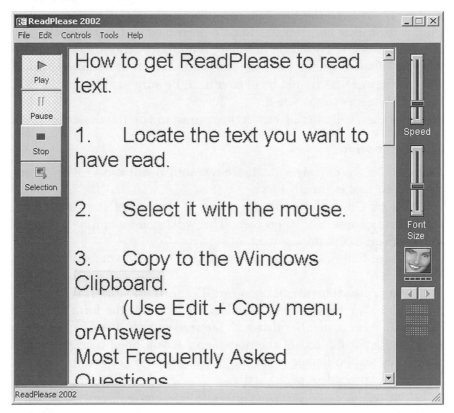

Figure 6-7. ReadPlease
When ReadPlease is first launched, instructions on using the program are located in the text window. Users should open a new document before pasting text into the window.

Finding and Installing

The ReadPlease Web site, www.readplease.com, has information about downloading the free version of the software, as well as the $49.95 Plus version and the $12.99 CD-ROM. Click on the link for ReadPlease 2002 Free, and then on the link for Download Now!. Users will need to provide their name and e-mail address before proceeding. Users are then given a choice of sites from which to download the tool. The WinSite selection will bring users to a page describing the system requirements and a link to start the download. The Simtel site requires users to choose a geographic area before beginning the download.

An executable icon will be downloaded to the desktop; double-clicking on it will begin the installation. Users will be given a choice to install either or both the free and the Plus versions of ReadPlease. The Plus version can be used 25 times before payment is required. The ReadPlease software will be installed, followed by the Microsoft Voice Engine. When installing the Microsoft component, users may be asked whether newer files should be overwritten. Be sure to click on the "No" button whenever this is asked.

ReadPlease will install icons in the systray and on the desktop.

Troubleshooting

Problem: I want to copy some more text into ReadPlease without erasing the text that is already there.

Solution: Go to the pulldown menu at the top of the ReadPlease screen and choose File, then New. This will open an empty document in which you can paste your text.

Problem: Rather than copy and paste text, can I open a document in ReadPlease?

Solution: ReadPlease can open text files (extension .txt). Word documents and Web pages can be saved as .txt files, but the formatting will be erased. Also remember that with the free version, ReadPlease has to start reading at the top of the document. If you open a large file and really only want a few pages in the middle to be read, you will have to listen to the preceding pages first.

Problem: Can I add pronunciations to ReadPlease?

Solution: Only with the Plus version can you add to the ReadPlease vocabulary. If you have this version, you can add a word to the reader's dictionary and provide a phonetic pronunciation for the reader's voice.

Problem: Can I change the size of the text in ReadPlease?

Solution: On the right-hand side of ReadPlease 2002 is a bar slide called Font Size that controls the size of the text. You can also adjust the speed of the reader with the bar slide called Speed.

Problem: I really need a PDF document to be read aloud.

Solution: Read the chapter on Adobe Access to see how to convert PDFs into text documents.

Library Uses

Any institution serving an older population or committed to providing access to people with visual impairments should investigate ways to improve access to online resources. Libraries looking for a free or low-cost screen reader should consider ReadPlease 2002. It is very easy to use, with a fairly natural sounding voice and a reputation for stability.

In addition to helping those with poor eyesight, ReadPlease has been reputed to help people with learning disabilities, particularly dyslexia. The program's method of highlighting each spoken word can be extremely beneficial to those with language disorders.

Chapter 7

Staff Tools for Librarians

OVERVIEW

Many librarians use the World Wide Web in a professional capacity. Reference questions may necessitate using search engines throughout the day to locate information. Interlibrary loan requests may be verified using Amazon.com and other online catalogs. Many library catalogs and e-mail systems are Web-based. It is the rare librarian who does not use the Web in some way during her workday.

The plug-ins listed in this chapter are tools that might not be appropriate for public access stations but could be very helpful to individuals. These tools modify the look of the browser or how it functions in such a way that might be confusing to the casual Web user. But for the librarian who wants a quicker way to conduct a Web search, or a safer way to use the mouse, or a more convenient way to eliminate pop-up and pop-under advertisements, these tools can be very beneficial. Librarians who do choose to use these plug-ins should be sure to educate others who share the workstation with them as to how the tools operate, and how to turn them off!

YAHOO! COMPANION AND GOOGLE TOOLBAR

Purpose

The Google Toolbar and Yahoo! Companion tools are both meant to enhance the functionality of the Web browser. Both seek to provide easy access to common Web browsing and searching functions. The Google Toolbar simply brings the features of www.google.com one step closer to the user. More personalization and customization are available on the Yahoo! Companion.

To use Yahoo! Companion successfully requires a Yahoo! account. The account allows each user to set preferences for display and functionality of the bar. Most of the features are not useful to librarians in their professional roles. However, some are handy shortcuts that may be useful to have at the reference desk.

System Requirements

GOOGLE TOOLBAR

Operating System: Windows 95 or later
Browsers: Internet Explorer 5.0 or later

YAHOO! COMPANION

Operating System: Windows 95 or later
Browsers: Internet Explorer 4.0 or later; Netscape 4.X

Internet Explorer 5.5 SP2 and 6.0 and Netscape 6.X Compatibility

Both Google Toolbar and Yahoo! Companion are compatible with later versions of Internet Explorer. However, neither will work with Netscape: Yahoo! Companion is incompatible, and the Google Toolbar only works with Internet Explorer.

Pros and Cons

The best feature of the two tools is the Google search box. Users can enter their search and get results without having the extra step of visiting the Google site. Although the time saved is minor, once users become accustomed to using the toolbar, the feature will seem invaluable.

The Google Toolbar also provides links to common Google search areas including the Google Web directory and newsgroup search. The Up button is a nice feature that will take users up one level in the current Web site, the equivalent of deleting the trailing end of the URL in the location bar to navigate backward through a site. Under the Page Info button, users will also find the feature Backward Links, which will display a list of pages that link to the page currently displayed in the browser window (to use this feature on www.google.com, use the search formula "link:URL").

Yahoo! Companion's most useful feature is the ability to save bookmarks. These bookmarks save to the Yahoo! user account and are then available from any computer with the Companion installed. The toolbar also links to common Yahoo! features including search, news, stock quotes and other finance information, movie and other entertainment information, and Yahoo! mail.

Since both tools install as an additional toolbar in the upper portion of the browser, they reduce the screen space available for Web pages. On large monitors, this should not be a problem. On smaller screens, however, the additional bar may an annoyance.

Examples

Figure 7-1. Google Toolbar
The Google Toolbar, shown above includes:

1) the Google logo, which provides links to standard Google searches,
2) the search box—users enter the terms they are looking for and hit the Enter key, which activates the next button,
3) the ability to search the Web,
4) if users select Search Site, the toolbar will search for the entered word within the current site,
5) PageRank, which indicates the popularity of the current site based on a complex formula that combines the number of times other Web sites link to the current site and the relative importance of those linking pages,
6) Up moves users up one level in the Web site's directory structure,
7) clicking on Highlight will highlight the search term entered by the user on the current Web page,
8) and the last list of keywords allows users to find single occurrences of the word on the current page.

Figure 7-2. Yahoo! Companion
Here the Yahoo! Companion is shown with the icons for Search, Bookmarks, Calendar, News, Yellow Pages, Maps, and Sign Off. Because the toolbar is so customizable, every user's toolbar will have different options in different order. Beside each icon, a pull-down menu arrow links to more options. For example, under the News icon, Headlines, Local News, Business, Sports, and Technology are some of the choices.

Finding and Installing

The Google Toolbar can be downloaded at toolbar.google.com. Users should visit the site with the browser in which they wish to install the toolbar. Select the desired language and click on Get the Google Toolbar! A pop-up window will appear warning users that by installing the advanced feature of the toolbar, the browser will send information to Google about the browsing habits of the user. Users who would prefer not to share their Web viewing habits with Google should be sure to install the toolbar without the advanced features. Answer Yes to the Security Warning pop-up box to complete the installation. If the toolbar does not appear at the top of the browser window, close and restart the browser.

To install the Yahoo! Companion, visit companion.yahoo.com. As with Google, users should visit with the browser in which they wish to install the toolbar. Click on the Get Yahoo! Companion button and answer Yes to the question on the Security Warning pop-up box. The toolbar should automatically install and appear at the top of the browser window. If the toolbar does not appear, users should restart their browsers.

Troubleshooting

Problem: I just installed Internet Explorer 6 and the Google Toolbar disappeared. How can I get it back?

Solution: First, go to the View menu, select Toolbars, and make sure that Google is checked. If this does not work, try to reinstall the toolbar.

Problem: The PageRank button does not appear in my Google Toolbar. How do I activate this feature?

Solution: When you installed the toolbar, you probably selected to turn off advanced features so that the toolbar wouldn't tell Google what Web site you are visiting. If you have changed your mind and would like to turn the advanced feature on, select the Toolbar Option item from the pull-down menu under the Google image on the toolbar. Check the PageRank display box under Advanced Features.

Problem: I'm using Netscape 4.6 on a Macintosh and I'd like to install the Yahoo! companion. Where can I download the tool?

Solution: Unfortunately, neither the Yahoo! Companion nor the Google Toolbar is currently available on the Macintosh platform.

Library Uses

The Google Toolbar would be useful on any desk in the library. Most librarians, especially those in reference, use the Web on a daily basis, and searching is an integral part of the job. At the reference desk, the Backward Links feature can be used to show patrons one method of checking the reliability of a page. Of course, checking backward links alone does not answer the question of whether a page is worthwhile, but checking for links to that page from other reliable sources can be a helpful determinant. PageRank works in a similar fashion.

Yahoo! Companion can be useful if a shared user account is set up and used at the reference desk. Bookmarks saved to the common account would then be accessible from any other stations in the library with the toolbar installed. The account can also be set up to recognize the library's physical location. The Yellow Pages, Maps, and Driving Directions features can then be used to identify and create printable maps to nearby locations such as post offices, banks, or public library branches. The Calendar feature could also be used to schedule library service desks for libraries that do not have commercial scheduling software packages available on their networks.

MOUSETOOL

Purpose

People who have some type of repetitive stress injury often find that using a computer mouse can irritate or even worsen the condition. Some computer users try different computer mouses until they find an ergonomically agreeable model. But for others, no mouse is comfortable. MouseTool is downloadable software that can ease discomfort for some users.

When navigating the Web, the computer mouse is indispensable. The easiest way to follow a hyperlink is by clicking with the mouse. This constant clicking with one finger can become painful, however. This is where MouseTool comes in. MouseTool runs in the background of the computer and works in any GUI program. The user moves the mouse to the desired location on the screen; when she pauses for a user-designated time, the left mouse button automatically clicks.

MouseTool also comes with a timer to remind computer users to take a stretch break every X number of minutes. Many ergonomics and repetitive stress experts promote the idea of taking frequent breaks away from the computer as a way to avoid or lessen computer injuries. All too often, a computer worker will become so involved with her work that she has no concept of time passing, never thinking to stop and stretch. A user who has set the MouseTool Stretch Break Timer will see a dialog box open in front of the active program window reminding her to take a break. After the user clicks on the "OK" button in the box, the reminder will disappear until it is time for the next break.

As mentioned, MouseTool can be used in programs like Microsoft Office or Adobe Photoshop, as well as in a browser. A user can set up "hotkeys" to indicate a double-clicking action of the mouse, and to enable the mouse to drag items around a screen without keeping the mouse button depressed.

System Requirements

Operating Systems: Windows 95 and higher
Browsers: Any graphical browser
File Size: 453 K

Pros and Cons

Many librarians spend a majority of their working day in front of a computer. As a result, our profession is at high risk for repetitive stress injuries such as carpal tunnel and tendonitis. MouseTool can bring significant relief to users who are suffering from pain in their hands and wrists from extended mouse use.

MouseTool can be frustrating to new users. There are relatively few "neutral" areas on a computer screen—that is, places where clicking the mouse upon them will not result in some action. Users must train themselves to think about where their cursor is, rather than being unaware until they want to click on something. A mouse cursor inadvertently paused on a link will send the user to another Web page she did not intend to visit at that moment. It can be especially disconcerting when viewing a page that is slow to download. A user may place the mouse in a seemingly empty part of a page, only to find that an image map has not yet been downloaded into the area; MouseTool will click on the momentarily invisible link, sending the user to another page, where there may be another link in that exact spot, sending the user to yet another place on the Web.

Users can set the options in MouseTool to dictate how long a mouse must be paused before it clicks. MouseTool can also be easily turned on and off by double-clicking on the tool's icon in the systray. This is especially beneficial for users who wish to use MouseTool selectively; a user can turn it on when surfing the Web, and then turn it off when writing text in Word or manipulating images in Photoshop.

Version 3.1 will most likely be the final one for this product; its creator has decided that supporting this tool is unfeasible for him. He has created a Linux version but has no plans for a Macintosh-compatible

MouseTool. A FAQ on the MouseTool Web site provides answers to the most frequent problems, but there is no formal customer support for this tool.

Examples

Figure 7-3. MouseTool's System Tray Icon
The systray, located in the lower right hand of the screen in Windows, includes icons for some programs. The MouseTool icon is in the middle and looks like a computer mouse. It flashes red when its clicking action is activated.

Figure 7-4. MouseTool's Menu
Right-clicking on the icon will bring up a set of options, including the ability to stop the tool. Under Options, users can set the dwell time and stretch break timer.

Figure 7-5. MouseTool's Prompter
The MouseTool Stretch Break Timer activates this dialog box after a set number of minutes dictated by the user.

Finding and Installing

MouseTool can be downloaded for a free 20-day trial from its Web site at www.mousetool.com. When the creator decided to cease support for MouseTool, he stopped charging for it and changed its designation to donationware: after the trial, users who wish to continue with the product should send $20 to the charity of their choice.

Troubleshooting

Problem: I've installed the donationware version, but it is asking me for a registration code.

Solution: According to the MouseTool site, the following codes can be used:

Name: MouseTool User
Code: HBBOBHILGBMMADMOPCMLCHPENPON

Problem: I'm having difficulties controlling the MouseTool.

Solution: The most common problem encountered is having the MouseTool click unexpectedly. This is mostly a user-training issue. You must learn to be more aware of the mouse, and particularly where you rest it on the screen. Safe places include the window bar at the top of the open program and directly on the scroll bars to the sides of the windows. Be certain you are resting the mouse in the active window! Most people find it easier to use MouseTool in a Web browser than when word processing.

Problem: The mouse is clicking faster or more often than I would like.

Solution: You can change the settings for MouseTool by right-clicking on the icon and choosing Options, then General. In this menu, you can set how long the mouse must be still before it clicks. Increase the number of seconds in the "Dwell Time" box if you want the pause between mouse movement and clicking to be longer. Also, double-check the systray and make certain there is only one MouseTool icon. If there are two or more icons, you have somehow started a second MouseTool on your computer. This can lead to confusion as each MouseTool tries to click. Right-click on the extra icons and choose "Stop MouseTool."

Problem: I want to use MouseTool for surfing the Web but not other programs.

Solution: Double-clicking the MouseTool icon in the systray will temporarily turn it off. Just double-click on the icon again to reactivate it.

Problem: I am a Mac user and would like to use MouseTool.

Solution: There are no plans to create a Mac version of this tool, but the creator of MouseTool recommends RJ Cooper's SmartClick, available from rjcooper.com/smartclick/index.html. This Mac-only tool works similarly to MouseTool, but costs $99.

Library Uses

MouseTool can be very helpful for individuals but incredibly confusing for anyone who unknowingly sits down at a computer with MouseTool turned on. It should not be installed on public stations, and cautiously on shared stations. Librarians who wish to have MouseTool on a shared computer, such as one situated at a reference desk, should alert colleagues and demonstrate how to turn the MouseTool on and off via the systray.

POP-UP STOPPER

Purpose

In an attempt to garner Web user attention, many advertisers have turned to pop-up advertisements as an alternative to banner ads. A user visiting a commercial site such as Yahoo will load the requested site, and then find a second, usually smaller window automatically loaded with advertising content has "popped up" either in front or behind the original site. Some sites, such as Amazon, use pop-ups to alert customers to specials like free shipping or upcoming sale dates.

Some users find this advertising strategy objectionable. Bandwidth can be eaten up as the browser has to load not only the requested site, but also the pop-up ad window. As the ads are often graphically intense, these files can be quite large. Additionally, users who are visually impaired and rely upon Web-text readers have difficulties as the readers become confused with the second window. And perhaps the majority of users simply find the constant pop-ups annoying.

Panicware's Pop-up Stopper aims to help by not allowing any new windows to open. The free version graphically flashes or plays a sound when a new browser window tries to open but is defeated. A professional version costs $19.95 and allows users to selectively choose pop-up ads in Internet Explorer.

System Requirements

Operating Systems: Windows 95 and higher (free version does not work in XP)
Browsers: Internet Explorer 5.X and higher; Netscape 4.X
File Size: 426 KB

Pros and Cons

Pop-up Stopper is extremely easy to install and run. Unlike some similar tools that force the user to maintain a list of banned content providers, this program automatically disallows all pop-ups.

This complete ban can be problematic at times. Clicking on a hyperlink that tries to load in a new window brings up a brief error message, then is defeated. The novice Pop-up Stopper user may be confused as to why a link appears not to work. Also, there are times when a user may want to open a new browser window. Pop-up stopper ignores the File->New->Window menu command, as well as the Control-N shortcut. Users can temporarily turn off Pop-up Stopper by double-clicking the icon in the systray, or they can hold down the Shift or Control key while clicking on a link or menu command. This will temporarily override the Stopper. Purchasing the professional version allows the manual opening of windows.

An argument could be made that some pop-ups contain useful information. Surveys, sales promotions, and alerts to visitors are often placed in pop-up windows. People with Pop-up Stopper may be missing important information.

Some users have complained that installation of Pop-up Stopper has caused their Internet Explorer to crash. This failure has not happened with enough consistency to nail down a reason for this problem. Many users with IE have no problem using Pop-up Stopper.

Pop-up Stopper is a nice, small utility because it has a specific purpose: forbidding the opening of new windows. It does not affect banner ads. Advertisers are constantly trying new ways to make an impact on the Web and will no doubt develop new ways to display ads that are not easily defeated.

Examples

Figure 7-6. Error Message Indicates Another Window Unsuccessfully Tried to Launch
Clicking on a hyperlink coded to open in a new browser window results in an error message.

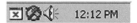

Figure 7-7. Pop-up Stopper's System Tray Icon
The "X" turns red when Pop-up Stopper is active and gray when it is disabled. It
briefly flashes when it stops a window from opening.

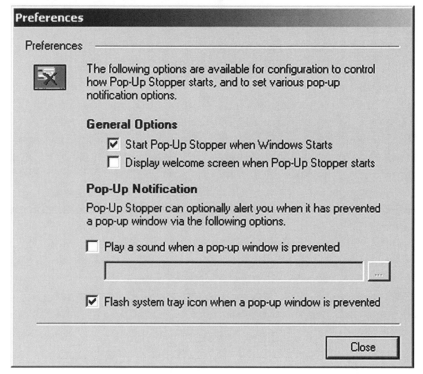

Figure 7-8. Pop-up Stopper's Preferences
The Preferences dialog box for Pop-up Stopper provides users with the opportunity to have the utility start automatically when they turn on their computers,
as well as decide if and how they would like to be notified when it prevents a
pop-up window.

Finding and Installing

Visit the Panicware site at www.panicware.com to download a free copy
of Pop-up Stopper. Although the company has a professional version for
sale, the site makes it easy to find a link to the free version. An executable file for Pop-up Stopper can be quickly downloaded to the computer.
Shut down all other programs before opening the .exe file. An installation wizard will guide the user through the set-up for Pop-up Stopper.

During the installation the user can decide whether to have the utility automatically open when Windows starts.

Like many plug-ins and Web tools, Pop-up Stopper installs an icon onto the systray. This icon is more useful than most, however. Double-clicking on this icon allows the user to toggle the utility on and off with ease.

TROUBLESHOOTING

Problem: I am using a current version of Internet Explorer but cannot get Pop-up Stopper to work.

Solution: First, make certain you are not using a "branded" version of IE. Branded versions have an icon of an ISP, such as Earthlink, in the upper right hand corner of the browser window.

If you are using a normal, stand-alone version of IE, it may need to be repaired. From the Start menu, go to Settings, Control Panel, Add/ Remove Programs. Select Internet Explorer, and choose Repair. Reboot your computer after repairing IE. This should fix the problems.

Problem: I want to open or allow a link to open in another browser window.

Solution: You can hold down the Shift or Control key while clicking on a link or instructing the browser to open another window. Sometimes, particularly with hyperlinks javascripted to open in a new window, this will not work. Double-clicking on the Pop-up Stopper icon in the systray will temporarily disable it. Double-click to turn it back on after the new window opens.

Problem: I need more help with this tool.

Solution: Panicware's Web site contains a FAQ for common questions about its products, including Pop-up Stopper. Panicware also provides free, unlimited technical support through e-mail. Go to the company's site for the most up-to-date e-mail address.

Library Uses

Although Pop-up Stopper might be ideal to solve some public access station problems, it would most likely create new ones. It would help in instances of unwanted pop-ups, particularly with pornographic sites that unleash numerous pop-ups when a user tries to back out of the adult sites. But it disables all pop-ups; sites like MEDLINEplus, which recommend reliable Web pages and arrange for the pages to open in new windows, would be impossible to use. All patrons would have to be taught how to disable the Pop-up Stopper.

Librarians who spend a great deal of time on the Web may enjoy Pop-up Stopper quite a bit. Many libraries use Amazon.com to confirm book information or Yahoo! to search throughout the day, and it becomes tiresome to close all the pop-up and pop-under windows that the homepages of these sites generate with each visit. Any librarians using a shared computer containing Pop-up Stopper need to be trained in turning the utility on and off, of course.

Chapter 8

Strategies for Managing Plug-Ins

OVERVIEW

After having installed all of the desired plug-ins and ActiveX controls, users must develop methods for managing all of their new software. How will they keep track of new versions? How can they deal with multiple plug-ins that are capable of playing the same file? What if they decide to remove a plug-in that is deemed redundant or unnecessary?

There are multiple methods for keeping track of plug-in updates. Users can maintain a bookmark or favorites folder that contains links to the homepages of each of the download software program sites. However, this takes time and a commitment on the users' part to faithfully check the sites. Some plug-ins helpfully alert users that a new version has been made available. However, users may find the frequent alerts from these programs annoying and turn the feature off. Another option is to identify a few good plug-in and ActiveX sites on the Web and monitor all of the tools from that site. Web sites for monitoring plug-ins and ActiveX controls are listed in Appendix C.

PLUGSY, PLUG MASTER, AND ACTIVEX MANAGER

Purpose

Plug-in and ActiveX control managers help users deal with a large number of installed browser tools. They provide information about which tools are running each file type, allow users to select and unselect (or turn off and on) tools, view information about the tools, and identify conflicts. Each of these three tools varies in the amount of control given to the user.

These programs help users by allowing an alternative to the browser-based plug-in managers. For Netscape, the built-in controls are located in the Preferences window, under Applications. Each file type name is listed, along with plug-in/helper application that handles the file, the file extension, and the MIME type. Removing files here is easy; users simply click the Remove button. Editing the file type allows users to select another program to run the file, as long as the program's path is known. Adding new file types is more difficult, requiring users to know the file extension, MIME type, and program location. Internet Explorer relies on the MIME type settings as defined by the operating system. Windows users can view the list by opening My Computer, selecting Folder Options (or Options), then choosing the tab for File Types.

System Requirements

PLUGSY

Processor:	Pentium PC
Operating Systems:	Windows 95 or greater
Browsers:	Any 32-bit browser that supports plug-ins

ACTIVEX MANAGER

Processor:	Pentium PC
Operating Systems:	Windows 95 or better
Browsers:	Any browser that supports ActiveX controls
File Size:	333KB

PLUG MASTER

Processor:	68K or PowerPC
Operating Systems:	System 7 or better
Browsers:	Any browser that supports plug-ins

Internet Explorer 5.5 SP2 and 6.0 and Netscape 6.X Compatibility

Since these programs run outside of the browser environment, the browser version is irrelevant. The important component is that the correct program is installed for the type of browser tools being used. For example, Windows users who run only Internet Explorer 6.0 will need ActiveX Manager. Windows users running only Netscape 4.76 will not require this tool; in this case, Plugsy would be the software to install.

Pros and Cons

Unlike most of the tools discussed in this book, these tools cost money. Plugsy and ActiveX Manager both cost $29.95 for a single user. Site licenses are also available. Both programs offer a 30-day evaluation download of their fully functional products. Users who use plug-ins and ActiveX controls will need both programs to manage their browser tools. Plug Master is shareware and costs $5 per user; site licenses are also available.

Plug Master, developed by independent software developer Mike Tilstra, is the most basic of the three programs. It allows users to identify installed plug-ins and turn them on or off. Users can identify individual plug-ins to turn off, or turn off the entire set at once. Turning off one plug-in helps users who have two plug-ins that play the same file type. Turning off one allows the desired plug-in to work with the file. After the file is played, the user can turn the temporarily unwanted plug-in back on. Macintosh users may notice that the software works very similarly to the Extensions Manager program that comes with System 7.5 and higher.

4Developers ActiveX Manager provides the next level of control. Users can view a list of all registered and unregistered ActiveX controls and turn on or off the desired control. For each selected control, users can view more information including the name, CLSID (for use in regedit), the location of the file on the users' system, the file size, and more. Controls may be viewed one at a time in the ActiveX Manager window or in a Web page report that the program can generate. The report can be customized to show only the information the user selects.

The program offering users the highest level of control is Digigami Plugsy. For each file format, Plugsy lists the DLL file of the program that plays it; allows users to get more information about the plug-in including name, version, release date, and a list of other file types the plug-in plays; and allows users to select another program to handle all files with that same extension. For example, if a user has both AlternaTIFF and QuickTime installed, QuickTime may set itself as the default player for all TIFF files. Using Plugsy, the user can override the settings and select AlternaTIFF as the default TIFF viewer without altering any of the other files QuickTime handles.

Examples

PLUGSY

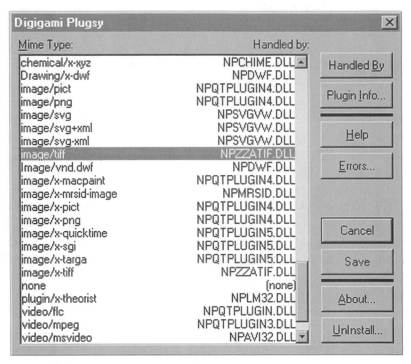

Figure 8-1. Plugsy
Plugsy displays each MIME type and the corresponding program that handles each type.

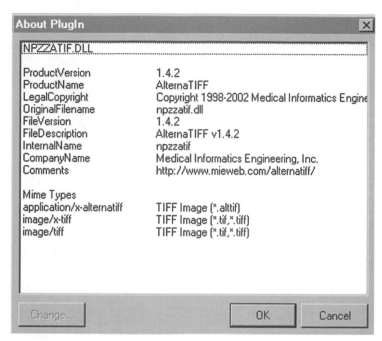

Figure 8-2. Plugin Info
Selecting Plugin Info displays a screen that provides details about the selected plug-in.

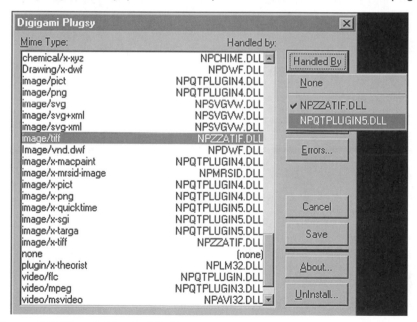

Figure 8-3. Plugsy's Handled By Button
The Handled By button allows users to select another program to handle this MIME type. In this example, QuickTime could be selected to replace AlternaTIFF as the default TIFF file viewer.

ACTIVEX MANAGER

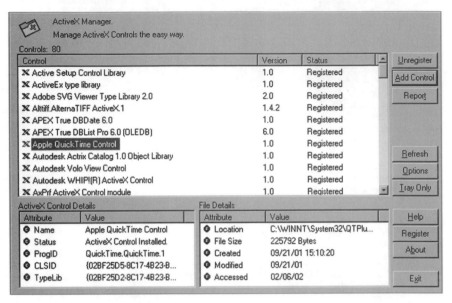

Figure 8-4. ActiveX Manager

The ActiveX Manager screen shows each control (in this case, only the Registered controls are visible), details about the control and about the control file.

Control Name: **Alttiff.AlternaTIFF ActiveX.1**
Version: 1.4.2
Status: Registered
File Location: C:\WINNT\Downloaded Program Files\alttiff.ocx
File Size: 450560 Bytes

Control Name: **IpixX ActiveX Control module**
Version: 6.2
Status: Registered
File Location: C:\WINNT\DOWNLO~1\ipixx.ocx
File Size: 102912 Bytes

Control Name: **CFSourceControl ActiveX Control module**
Version: 1.0
Status: Registered
File Location: C:\WINNT\System32\CFSOUR~1.OCX
File Size: 90112 Bytes

Control Name: **Shockwave ActiveX Control**
Version: 1.0
Status: Registered
File Location: C:\WINNT\SYSTEM32\Macromed\Director\SwDir.dll
File Size: 32768 Bytes

Figure 8-5. ActiveX Manager Report
To view information about all of the controls at once, use ActiveX Manager to produce a report in HTML. For this report, Name, Version, Status, Location, and File Size were selected.

PLUG MASTER

Figure 8-6. Plug Master Group Management
Plug Master users define their own plug-in groups from the file menu.

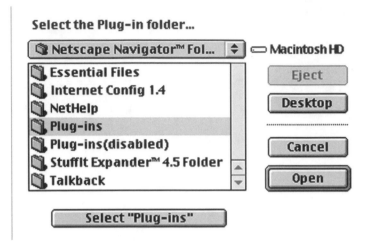

Figure 8-7. Plug-In Folder Selection
Each plug-in group points to a location on the hard drive where plug-ins are located. If plug-ins reside in more than one folder, each folder should get its own Plug Master plug-in group.

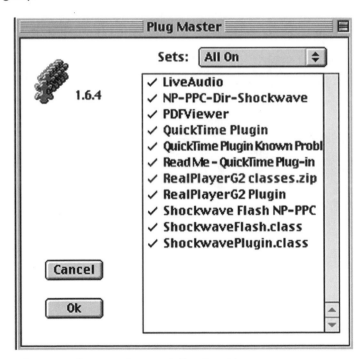

Figure 8-8. Turning Plug-Ins On and Off in Plug Master
Each plug-in in the folder can be turned off and on by clicking on the name. Users may also turn off and on all plug-ins with the pull-down menu at the top of the screen.

Finding and Installing

Plugsy: www.digigami.com/plugsy/download.html
ActiveX Manager: 4developers.com/xmgr
Plug Master: www.macupdate.com/info.php/id/380
Each of the three programs will download a file to the user's hard drive. Double-clicking on the downloaded file will install the software.

Troubleshooting

Problem: The only program listed under the WAV file type in Plugsy is QuickTime. How do I select WinAMP as the program I want to play this file? I'm using Netscape 4.

Solution: Unfortunately, this cannot be done from within Plugsy. However, Plugsy can make the job easier. First write down the file extension and MIME type. Then make sure your browser is closed and in Plugsy under Handled By, select None. Then reopen the Web browser and go to the Applications section under Preferences. Create a New Type and fill out the sections for MIME type and file extension, then browse your system for WinAMP. The WinAMP program will now be listed under the Handled By list in Plugsy.

Problem: There are lots of controls shown in my ActiveX Manager list. What do all of these controls do?

Solution: ActiveX controls are used by Windows to control many system functions related to Web browsing. Most of the controls listed are for functions that happen behind the scenes. When you are looking at the list, browse for familiar sounding names. The controls that are most important to you will have recognizable names such as Shockwave ActiveX control or Real Player ActiveX control Library. For the most part, the other controls can be ignored.

Library Uses

Library staff members who use many plug-ins, helper applications, or ActiveX controls on their desktop machines may find the management tools helpful. System administrators may use them to help maintain the tools on the public stations. However, these programs should not be made available to the public user. If users are allowed to make changes in what programs run file types, each system in the library would have unique settings, making maintenance of the machines difficult. The system administrator should determine the best tools to optimize performance and then lock down access to these management tools.

UNINSTALLING PLUG-INS

It is unwise for users on Windows or Macintosh machines to delete programs by dragging the program folder to the Recycle Bin or to the Trash. Although this will make it so that users are unable to run the program, it leaves behind other files that are scattered throughout the system. The proper method for uninstalling programs is outlined below.

Windows

METHOD 1: ADD/REMOVE PROGRAMS

The first option to properly remove software is to use the Add/Remove Programs feature located on the Control Panel. From the Start menu, select Settings, then Control Panel. The Add/Remove Programs box includes most of the software installed on the system. Look for the program to delete, highlight it, then click on Add/Remove and follow the steps on the screen.

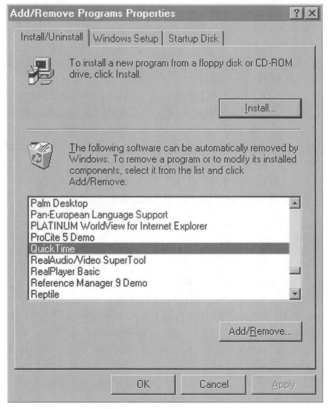

Figure 8-9. Add/Remove Programs
If the program does not appear in the list, try the next option.

METHOD 2: PROGRAM UNINSTALLER

Another way to properly uninstall software is to run the uninstaller that was installed along with the program. The easiest way to access the uninstaller is to find the program in the Start menu, select it, and look for the Uninstall option.

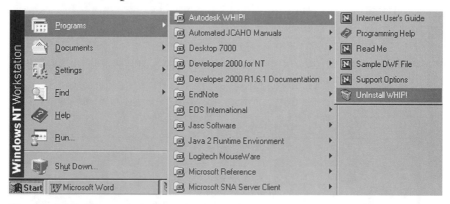

Figure 8-10. Uninstalling from the Start Menu
In this example, Whip! installed its own uninstall feature. Selecting this option will remove the program and all of its components from the system.

METHOD 3: UNINSTALL SOFTWARE

Another option is to purchase software designed to completely clean the system when programs are uninstalled. These programs are better about cleaning out the Windows Registry than the methods above and they also help prevent the accidental removal of files that are needed by another program. The two most popular commercial products are McAfee's UnInstaller and Norton CleanSweep.

CleanSweep can be purchased from Symantec at www.symantec.com/sabu/ncs, and costs $29.95. It is also available at online and brick-and-mortar software retailers.

UnInstaller is available in two formats: on CD-ROM or online. The CD-ROM version can be purchased from software retailers for the suggested cost of $19.95. At the McAfee Web site, users may sign up for UnInstallerOnline, an Application Service Provider (ASP) version that users purchase by subscription and install from the Internet. McAfee requires users to sign up for the service (currently $19.95/year) and install the plug-in or ActiveX control. The subscription allows users unlimited access to the software, including upgrades, for the length of the subscription. Unfortunately, UnInstallerOnline is incompatible with Netscape Navigator 6. More information is available at www.mcafee.com/myapps/muo/default.asp.

Macintosh

Uninstalling software on a Macintosh is more straightforward. In addition to dragging the appropriate application folder to the Trash, users should check for components installed in the System Folder, Control Panels Folder, Extensions Folder, and the Preferences Folder. Some applications will not have files to remove in all of these folders, while others, such as QuickTime, will deposit files in all of the folders.

After removing all of the files found, users should use the Fast Find feature and search for the application name to find any stragglers and remove them as well.

Figure 8-11. System Folder

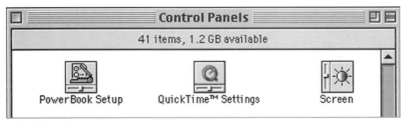

Figure 8-12. Control Panels Folder

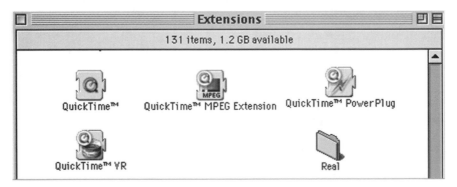

Figure 8-13. Extensions Folder

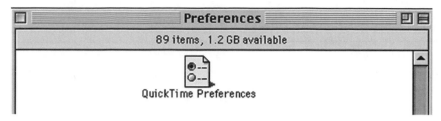

Figure 8-14. Preferences Folder

File Extensions:
The Guide to Extensions and
the Programs that Play Them

Plug-in	File Extension
Adobe Acrobat	PDF
AlternaTIFF	TIF, TIFF
Chime	CSM, CSME, CUB, EMB, EMBL, GAU, JDX, MOL, MOL2, MOP, PDB, RXN, SCR, SKC, SPT, TGF, XYZ
Cn3D	VAL
Excel Viewer	XLS, XLT, XLW
iPIX	AUT, BUB, IPS, IPX
LiveMath	THE, THP
MrSID	SID
PowerPoint Viewer	PPS, PPT
QuickTime	AIF, AIFC, AIFF, AU, AVI, BMP, DLS, DMF, DV, FLC, FLI, FLIC, FPX, GIF, JPEG, JPG, KAR, MID, MIDI, MOV, MP3, MPEG, MPG, PCS, PCT, PIC, PICT, PLS, PNG, PNT, PNTG, QT, QTM, QTVR, SF2, SGI, SND, TARGA, TGA, TIF, TIFF, WAV
RasMol	CRD, ENT, MOL, MOL2, MOP, PDB, SPT, XYZ
RealOne	AIF, AIFF, ASF, AVI, CDA, GIF, JPEG, JPG, LQT, MED, MES, MID, MIDI, MIF, MP3, MPEG, MPG, PNG, RA,

	RAM, RM, RMI, RP, RT, SMI, SMIL, SWF, WAV, WMA
Shockwave	AAM, DCR, DIR, DXR, SPL, SWA, SWF
Volo View	DWF, DWG, DXF, IAM, IDW, IPT
Whip!	DWF
WinAMP	AS, ASFS, CDA, IT, MID, MIDI, MOD, MP2, MP3, S3M, VOC, WAV, WMA, XM
Windows Media Player	AIF, AIFC, AIFF, ASF, ASX, AU, AVI, MID, MIDI, MP3, MPEG, MPG, RMI, VOD, WAV, WAX, WMA, WMD, WMS, WMV, WMZ, WVX
Word Viewer	DOC, DOT, RTF

File Extension	Plug-in
AAM	Shockwave
AIF, AIFC, AIFF	QuickTime, RealOne, Windows Media Player
AS, ASFS	WinAMP
ASF	RealOne, Windows Media Player
ASX	Windows Media Player
AU	QuickTime, Windows Media Player
AUT	iPIX
AVI	QuickTime, RealOne, Windows Media Player
BMP	QuickTime
BUB	iPIX
CDA	RealOne, WinAMP
CRD	Chime
CSM, CSME	Chime
CUB	Chime
DCR	Shockwave
DIR	Shockwave
DLS	QuickTime
DMF	QuickTime
DOC	Word Viewer
DOT	Word Viewer
DV	QuickTime
DWF	Volo View, Whip!
DWG	Volo View

DXF	Volo View
DXR	Shockwave
EMB, EMBL	Chime
ENT	RasMol
FLC	QuickTime
FLI, FLIC	QuickTime
FPX	QuickTime
GAU	Chime
GIF	QuickTime, RealOne
IAM	Volo View
IDW	Volo View
IPS	iPIX
IPT	Volo View
IPX	iPIX
IT	WinAMP
JDX	Chime
JPEG, JPG	QuickTime, RealOne
KAR	QuickTime
LQT	RealOne Player
MED	RealOne Player
MES	RealOne Player
MID, MIDI	QuickTime, RealOne, WinAMP, Windows Media Player
MIF	RealOne Player
MOD	WinAMP
MOL, MOL2	Chime, RasMol
MOP	Chime, RasMol
MOV	QuickTime
MP2	WinAMP
MP3	QuickTime, RealOne, WinAMP, Windows Media Player
MPEG, MPG	QuickTime, RealOne, Windows Media Player
PCS	QuickTime
PCT	QuickTime
PDB	Chime, RasMol
PDF	Adobe Acrobat Reader
PIC, PICT	QuickTime
PLS	QuickTime
PNG	QuickTime, RealOne
PNT, PNTG	QuickTime
PPS	PowerPoint Viewer

PPT	PowerPoint Viewer
QT	QuickTime
QTM	QuickTime
QTVR	QuickTime
RA, RAM, RM, RMI	RealOne
RMI	Windows Media
RP	RealOne
RT	RealOne
RTF	Word Viewer
RXN	Chime
S3M	WinAMP
SCR	Chime
SF2	QuickTime
SGI	QuickTime
SID	MrSID
SKC	Chime
SMI, SMIL	RealOne
SND	QuickTime
SPL	Shockwave
SPT	Chime, RasMol
SWA	Shockwave
SWF	RealOne, Shockwave
TARGA, TGA	QuickTime
TGF	Chime
THE	LiveMath
THP	LiveMath
TIF, TIFF	QuickTime, AlternaTIFF
VAL	Cn3D
VOC	WinAMP
VOD	Windows Media Player
WAV	QuickTime, RealOne, WinAMP, Windows Media Player
WAX	Windows Media Player
WMA	RealOne, WinAMP, Windows Media Player
WMD	Windows Media Player
WMS	Windows Media Player
WMV	Windows Media Player
WMZ	Windows Media Player
WVX	Windows Media Player
XLS	Excel Viewer

XLT	Excel Viewer
XLW	Excel Viewer
XM	WinAMP
XYZ	Chime, RasMol

Appendix B

Troubleshooting Tips:
The Guide to Common Problems
and All-Purpose Solutions

If you are having difficulties with a plug-in, here are some common, all-purpose solutions that may help.

Upgrade the plug-in. Visit the plug-in's Web site and install the newest version available. Often, the most recently created files will be tailored to the latest version of the plug-in and are not backwards compatible.

Uninstall older versions of the plug-in. Different versions of the tool may be conflicting with each other.

Upgrade the browser. Some plug-ins work best with the Internet Explorer 5.5 or 6.0. Also, plug-ins that do not work in Netscape Navigator 6.0 sometimes have success with Netscape 6.2.

Try the "other" browser. Sometimes a plug-in will only work with the browser with which it was downloaded, and when the other browser is used, the plug-in cannot be invoked.

Upgrade the hardware. Audio problems can often be traced to old sound cards and problematic drivers.

Install one plug-in at a time. This way, you can isolate troublemakers and take the necessary steps to correct the problems. It is much more difficult when you are unsure which tool is the culprit.

Search the Web for answers. Use your favorite search engine, troll usenet groups, and scour the support sections of plug-in sites for answers. Web4Lib Archives (listed in Appendix C) is an excellent source of information from fellow librarians.

Appendix C

Webliography:
The Guide for Learning About and
Locating the Right Programs

PLUG-IN SITES

ActiveX Manager
4developers.com/xmgr

Adobe Access
access.adobe.com

Adobe Acrobat Reader
www.adobe.com

AlternaTIFF
www.alternatiff.com

Chime
www.mdlchime.com/chime

Cn3D
www.ncbi.nlm.nih.gov/Structure/CN3D/cn3dinstall.shtml

Google Toolbar
toolbar.google.com

iPIX viewer
www.ipix.com

Lens Magnifying Glass
www.abfsoftware.com

LiveMath
www.livemath.com

Microsoft Office Viewers
office.microsoft.com/downloads/default.aspx

MrSID
www.lizardtech.com

MouseTool
www.mousetool.com

Plug Master
www.macupdate.com/info.php/id/380

Plugsy
www.digigami.com/plugsy/download.html

Pop-up Stopper
www.panicware.com

QuickTime
www.apple.com/quicktime

RasMol
www.umass.edu/microbio/rasmol/getras.htm

ReadPlease
www.readplease.com

RealOne
www.real.com

Shockwave
www.macromedia.com

Volo View Express
www.autodesk.com

Whip!
www.autodesk.com

WinAMP
www.winamp.com

Windows Media Player
www.microsoft.com/windows/windowsmedia

Yahoo! Companion
companion.yahoo.com

HELPFUL SITES

CNET
www.cnet.com
Find articles, downloads, and news items.

Netscape Browser Plug-in Finder
home.netscape.com/plugins
Click on "Find Plug-ins" in left-hand bar to get to a search screen.
Choose your platform and what type of file you want supported, and
Netscape will tell you which plug-ins you need.

Tucows
www.tucows.com
Excellent resource for downloading software, especially older versions
of plug-ins.

Web4Lib Archives
sunsite.berkeley.edu/Web4Lib/archive.html
The archive for this electronic discussion list, designed for librarians with
an interest in the Web, has a great search engine.

Index

About the Authors

Candice M. Benjes-Small received her master's degree in library and information science from the University of Texas at Austin. She is currently a reference and instruction librarian at Radford University in Virginia. Previously, she was a Webmaster for the University of Southern California's Norris Medical Library. She has given presentations and written articles about the Web, including Web site usability testing. Her paper, "Balancing on the Bleeding Edge: Making the Right Choices with Cool Tools," presented at the Internet Librarian Conference in 2000, was the inspiration for this book.

Melissa L. Just is an information specialist at the University of Southern California's Norris Medical Library and the manager of the Health Sciences Library at Children's Hospital Los Angeles. She has managed library Web sites and intranets and presented, published, and taught on the topic of Web authoring and site development. Melissa received her master's of library and information science degree from the University of Texas at Austin and is currently pursuing an educational doctorate at the University of Southern California.